# Age
## PROOFING

7 simple
steps to
super vitality
at any age

Robert D. Willix Jr., M.D., F.A.C.S.M.

# NOTICE

This book is intended as a reference volume only, not as a medical manual. The information given here is designed to help adults make informed decisions about their health. It is not intended as a substitute for any treatment that may have been prescribed by your doctor. You should consult your physician before beginning an exercise program or a vitamin and supplement regimen. Women who are pregnant or are considering becoming pregnant or who are nursing should consult their doctor before embarking on a new exercise or supplement regimen. If you suspect that you have a medical problem, we urge you to seek competent medical help.

AGEproofing
7 Simple Steps to Super Vitality at Any Age

Written by Robert D. Willix, Jr.

Cover design: Bren Frisch
Illustrations: Susan Strawn Bailey

PRINTING HISTORY
2000

For information contact:
Real Health Books
243 E. Fourth St.
Loveland, CO 80537

PRINTED IN THE UNITED STATES OF AMERICA
10 9 8 7 6 5 4 3

# Acknowledgements

There are so many people to thank for the publishing of *AGEproofing* that I hardly know where to begin.

I will start with Judith Strauss, my copy editor, without whom this manuscript could not have taken its present form. We have worked together for over six years. Each year she amazes me with the depth of her kindness and spirit.

Susan Clotfelter, from the start, was an inspiration and now a new friend. Her attention to detail has brought *AGEproofing* to a much higher level.

There will never be a way that I can express my gratitude to my friend and executive assistant Robin Weinstein. She is always there when I need her and finds a way to get the job done on time, no matter what the obstacle. There is no possible limit to her many talents.

Thank you to all the people at Real Health Books and Herb Companion Press —Ceri Anderson, Dean Howes, Kelli Rosen, Amy Baugh-Meyer, and Marci Jackson—who put long, hard hours into this book to make it a quality book.

There were so many inspirational teachers in my career. I appreciate and applaud all of you. I hope we will never underestimate the influence of the teachers that have molded our lives. My mentor at the University of Michigan, Herbert Sloan, M.D.; my friend and inspiration George Sheehan M.D.; the pioneers of alternative medicine, Deepak Chopra, M.D. and Bernie Siegal, M.D.; and the great thinkers Albert Einstein and R.W. Emerson; all have contributed to this book.

Finally, I owe my gratitude to Logan Chamberlain, Ph.D., who inspired me to take on this challenge.

My prayers are with all of you. I know that God will bring blessing upon you.

Robert D. Willix, Jr., M.D.

## DEDICATION

To my parents, Robert D. Willix, Sr., and Natalie C. Willix, who taught me to never accept mediocrity and to live out my dreams. Thank you!

*And*

To my wife Donna Lee. Your perpetual smile and your ability to grow and change have been inspirational. You allow me to explore new challenges; now it is time for you to do the same.

# CONTENTS

Introduction
by John Douillard, Ph.D. . . . . . . . . . . . . . . . . . . . . . . . .I

Chapter 1:
    My Journey to Health—and Yours  . . . . . . . . . . . .1

Chapter 2:
    Smashing the Age Barrier  . . . . . . . . . . . . . . . . . .19

Chapter 3:
    The Commitment to Change  . . . . . . . . . . . . . . .35

Chapter 4:
    Step 1—Assessing Your Risks  . . . . . . . . . . . . . .53

Chapter 5:
    Step 2—Aerobics . . . . . . . . . . . . . . . . . . . . . . . .73

Chapter 6:
    Step 3—Antioxidants . . . . . . . . . . . . . . . . . . . .105

Chapter 7:
    Step 4—Managing Stress . . . . . . . . . . . . . . . . . .135

Chapter 8:
    Step 5—Strength Training  . . . . . . . . . . . . . . . .163

Chapter 9:
    Step 6—Keeping Your Flexibility  . . . . . . . . . . .185

Chapter 10:
    Step 7—Nutritional Balance  . . . . . . . . . . . . . . .215

Epilogue . . . . . . . . . . . . . . . . . . . . . . . . . . . . . . . .257

# Introduction
## by John Douillard, Ph.D.

In this fascinating book, Dr. Willix shows us how simple it is to live up to our human potential. Though our society typically considers life spans of 125 years to be impossible—or possible only for members of exotic societies hidden away in remote, nearly unreachable parts of the world—Dr. Willix shows us how to bring the reality of longevity right into our own lives.

It is no secret that we are functioning at a fraction of our capabilities—mentally and physically. Researchers tell us that we use only about one one-hundredth of one percent of our full potential. We accomplish this undistinguished feat through a lifestyle fraught with exhaustion and stress. We typically push ourselves to the point of collapse in a relentless, neverending drive to do and have more. Obviously, this approach to life cannot provide a sense of happiness or well-being.

Dr. Willix not only paves the way for us to remove such stressors from our lives, he also shows us how to change our ways so that we don't incur the stressors in the first place. The amazing result is that Dr. Willix shows us how to extend our life spans (which is the hallmark of this book), while he shows us how to dramatically improve the quality of life in terms of health and happiness. And this is of major importance. After all, no one wants to live a long life in a barely functional state, farmed out to a nursing home.

After reading this book, you will not fear the future. Rather, you will see it as a time to gracefully age, full of energy and in good health, sharing the wisdom of a lifetime with your children and grandchildren.

In our society, the deterioration that we equate with old

age has made us lose respect for those who, in traditional cultures, have always been the most highly revered. As we learn how to be healthy at 100, the dignity of growing old will be restored to us. With that, the elders of our society will regain their rightful place as our leaders.

In *AGEproofing*, Dr. Willix has blended the scientific findings of the West with the ancient wisdom of the East—where old age is still venerated—better than anyone I have yet seen. He uses scientific proofs as well as centuries-old evidence from other cultures to make an incredibly good case for our potential to extend the current human life span. And he recognizes that today, an intelligent approach to longevity has to include an understanding of the modern lifestyle, plus everything that modern researchers have learned about exercise and nutrition, along with the time-honored techniques of the Orient.

The ancient wisdom that Dr. Willix draws upon has passed the test of time. Ayurvedic medicine, for example, is one of the oldest systems of medicine in the world. Not only that, it is today, as we speak, also one of the biggest. Over 300,000 Ayurvedic practitioners belong to the All Indian Ayurvedic Congress, while the American medical Association has only about 250,000 doctors as members. And traditional Chinese medicine is still the mainstay of the medical system in China, the largest country in the world.

Dr. Willix reminds us that the world is a huge place with a vast reservoir of knowledge. That the Western way is not the only way, and that there is something for us to learn from all systems of medicine still being practiced today— the biggest and the oldest, as well as the newest and most highly technical. In *AGEproofing*, he has connected all this information, and has demystified the ancient wisdom by validating it with modern scientific studies.

What Dr. Willix has created here is a must read for people of all ages. His premise is prevention—the prevention of disease and debility—and that it's never too early to begin or too late to start enjoying life. If you follow the prescription that Dr. Willix sets forth in this book, you will be effortlessly charting a positive course for the rest of your life.

*John Douillard, Ph.D., is the author of* The Three-Season Diet *(Harmony, 2000) and the* Invincible Athletics *tape series. He is currently in private Ayurvedic practice in Boulder, Colorado.*

# CHAPTER 1

# MY JOURNEY TO HEALTH—AND YOURS

◆

*IMAGINE being able to jog at full speed when you're 70. Celebrating your 80th by making love with your spouse. Snow skiing instead of playing shuffleboard when you're 90. Imagine bounding out of bed in the morning— whether you're 55 or 105—and greeting the sunrise with a yoga stretch, then enjoying an active, pain-free, energy-filled day. All of these things, and more, are possible for you if you follow my simple program for good health at any age.*

*But first, you have to learn what you thought you knew about aging is as false as what you thought you knew about the inevitability of dying at age 75. You have to learn the truth that I discovered when I looked down at one of my cardiac surgery patients and saw my own future staring back up at me.*

◆

One day in the operating room I had a revelation that changed my life, both personally and professionally.

It was 1977. I was preparing to replace arteries in a patient's heart. I looked down on that table and saw this poor guy with his chest sawed open, and realized that this was not the answer.

He was no different from many other patients: over-weight, overworked, a smoker, somewhere between 45 and 55 years old. I knew that, after surgery, chances are he would return home and go right back to doing what it was that made him sick in the first place.

Because that's what most of my patients did. Many of them wound up in my operating room two and three times to undergo the same harrowing multiple bypass surgeries. Only each time, the risks got higher.

I realized at that moment that I was doing little or nothing to make my patients healthy. I was simply pro-longing their deaths. I knew I had to find a better way to help them.

## A frightening look in the mirror

At the same time, I realized that I was headed down the same road as my patients. Driven to succeed, I was work-ing more than 100 hours a week, smoking a pack and a half of cigarettes a day, and chowing down on 12-ounce steaks for dinner. The only exercise I got was picking up a scalpel.

While my medical practice was growing, so was my body. At age 34 and a height of 5 feet, 10 inches, I weighed 235 pounds. My life was out of my control. I knew that if I continued on this road, someday soon I'd be the guy on the table with my chest sawed open.

And when I learned that the average thoracic surgeon died between the ages of 54 and 56, it looked like I was right on track to becoming no more than another medical statistic.

## How I got to be unhealthy

Like most Americans in my generation, I was digging my early grave the old fashioned way: hard work.

I grew up on the streets of New Jersey, wanting nothing more than to play sports. I had visions of myself as a college football star—maybe even a pro. With that goal in mind, I headed for Boston College.

I majored in biology, with no idea of how I could put a biology degree to good use. I also tried to win a walk-on spot on the Boston College football team. At the end of a year of being pummeled mercilessly by 260-pound linemen, I realized I wasn't going to play varsity ball. I'd better concentrate on academics and not athletics.

A biochemistry professor talked me into applying for a graduate school fellowship. As a teaching fellow at Seton Hall University, I learned to love research. I published four articles in scientific journals, was awarded a fellowship from the National Institutes of Health, finished tops in my class, and was invited to transfer to medical school. Reasoning that I could earn my Ph.D. in biology along with an M.D., I accepted.

## The makings of a doctor

Halfway through my Ph.D. program, the four individuals responsible for overseeing my progress left to pursue their own careers. I had no choice but to transfer to a new medical school. I chose the University of Missouri.

From the moment I entered the clinical realm of medicine in my junior year, I fell in love with the pursuit of medical knowledge. At that point, I chose to concentrate fully on medicine instead of splitting myself between

## The Nurse Who Healed Herself

A 56-year-old nurse entered my program a few years ago. Her history was very simple. She had suffered from high blood pressure for 20 years, weighed 185 pounds, and had 35 percent body fat (20 to 22 percent is optimal for women.) She was taking three medications to control her blood pressure. She was taking another drug to control diabetes brought on by the blood pressure medications. And she was taking a fifth medication to prevent heart failure.

Three months after entering my program, she was down to 160 pounds. She exercised in the rehabilitation program 3-4 days a week, learned biofeedback and stress management, and reduced the carbohydrates and fat in her diet. She no longer had to take the diabetes and heart failure drugs. She was able to drop two of the blood-pressure prescriptions and cut the dosage on the remaining one by half. She brought her diabetes under control with what I taught her about alternatives to drug therapy.

medicine and biology research. This is a decision I've never regretted. To this day, I have not found anything more fulfilling than being able to help people feel better and healthier and more vibrantly alive.

As any doctor can tell you, however, medical school is a pressure cooker. My personal pressures increased when I got married and started a family. True to my upbringing and the work ethic I learned from my father, I told myself that I could cope if I just worked harder and worked more hours. So I went to medical school, worked nights as a security guard, and spent any remaining hours doing my research.

I believed the fallacy that the human body can get by on a mere three hours of sleep a day. The only thing that kept me going during this period was that my physical condition was excellent—the result of my years as a college athlete.

Finally, I graduated with honors from medical school. And there I was—an Irish-Italian kid from the streets of New Jersey—the first one in my family to get past high school—calling myself a doctor.

## Coping with growing demands

I began surgical training at the University of Michigan. By this time, our second child had been born, I had accumulated more than $60,000 in educational debt, and the university was paying me the princely sum of $5,900 a year to be a surgical intern.

I moved through my residency, working longer and longer hours. The horror stories you've heard about the demands of medical training are not exaggerations. At one point during my residency, one of my children actually told his playmates that I was dead simply because he had not seen me for three months.

The mix of intense competition, constant lack of sleep, unremitting scrutiny from professors of medicine and surgery, and continual financial worries creates serious problems for aspiring physicians. The result, at worst, can be depression (even suicide), drug and alcohol dependency, and mistakes in judgment that can cost patient lives. It can also lead to family problems and divorce, which is what happened in my case.

In 1973, as my marriage was ending and I was facing becoming a single parent with three children to raise, I began to understand that my career could endanger my own health. I was forced to begin making a few changes in how I lived. I discovered it was okay for me to read a book that had nothing to do with medicine, that it was okay to sleep for eight hours a night—and that I could do both if I forced myself to free up time away from work. I even started listening to music again, just for pleasure.

Still, this was a difficult time as I struggled to complete my residency and raise my children. I was overwhelmed by my responsibilities, and I wasn't paying nearly enough attention to my own well-being.

Finally, in 1975, I completed my post-graduate surgical training at the University of Michigan. From there I moved to Sioux Falls, South Dakota, where I became the first board-certified cardiac surgeon in the state, and began its first open-heart surgery program. I also taught at the University of South Dakota Medical School, then in its infancy.

## Running my way back to health

When I had my revelation in the operating room, I had been working in South Dakota for two years. A friend of mine, Dr. Larry Seidenstein, encouraged me to exercise, both as a way to lose weight and to reduce job-related stress. At his urging, I entered a three-mile race, realizing that I was about to make my first real attempt at purely physical activity since college eight years ago.

One week before the race, I thought I'd warm up by running a mile. Imagine my surprise when I discovered that it was all I could do to run about 20 yards, then walk 50 yards, then run, then walk, just so that I could make it through the mile.

The following week, I did manage to pant my way through the race. But afterwards, I felt so weak that I could barely drive the 70 miles back home. Disgusted with myself, I proclaimed for all to hear: "I'll never be unfit again!" And I meant it.

I began jogging on a regular basis, and the improvements came quickly. My weight dropped to 165 pounds, and within six months I ran my first marathon, a distance of 26.2 miles, along with my 63-year-old father. My father, by the way, had only taken up running in his 60s. He finished the marathon about six minutes before me, and crossed the finish line invigorated. It was all I could do to collapse across the line.

But I didn't give up, and eventually, in 1984, I fulfilled one of my dreams by going to Hawaii and competing in the IRONMAN Triathlon, a three-part athletic event that combines a 2.4-mile swim, a 112-mile bike ride, and a 26.2-mile run. At that point, only four thousand of us in the world had ever completed the IRONMAN.

## Changing myself, changing medicine

When I was in medical school, I spent only about four hours actual clock time studying the effect of nutrition on the human body—and even less time on the effects of exercise or stress management. In those years, such factors were simply not considered to be important for good health.

But as I continued my own quest, I learned just how critical these elements are to keeping healthy. I learned more and more about the benefits of a high-fiber diet and became a lacto-ovo-vegetarian (one that consumes dairy and eggs) in 1977. I began a regular program of stress management. As I continued to exercise and change my habits, I felt better and better.

I began a cardiac rehabilitation program to teach patients with heart disease what I had learned about exercise,

### LEARNING FROM MY PATIENTS' SUCCESSES

## Using Imagery To Clean An Artery

A 50-year-old builder came into my office one day after he had been exercising. My secretary called me immediately because he looked so ill. To make a long story short, we put him on a stretcher and he immediately went into a fatal type of arrhythmia known as ventricular fibrillation. I performed CPR until the paramedics came and we could do electrical counter-shock.

During his resuscitation, I kept telling him, "It's not time for you to leave—come back now." He says he still remembers going toward a white light, hearing my voice tellling him to come back—and then turning around, away from the white light, and coming back into his body.

This was only the beginning of this patient's journey into mind-body medicine. That same day, he was taken to the hospital where a cardiac catheterization revealed that he needed angioplasty or open-heart surgery to clear an artery that was nearly blocked.

While his irregular heartbeats were being stabilized in preparation for surgery, I went to the hospital to see him. I asked if he understood what his tests had nutrition, and stress management. In all my years of surgically replacing blood vessels in damaged hearts, I had never taught my patients to change themselves. But now I knew that surgery was a waste of time if it wasn't accompanied by a commitment to a healthier way of living. And I wanted patients to know, too.

shown, and then I described his lesions to him and taught him a mind-body technique known as self-hypnosis with imagery. He spent many of the next 36 hours imagining that he was traveling with his mind into his blocked artery and that he was clearing it out with an instrument he used in his building profession.

Much to the amazement of his cardiologist, when doctors again inserted the cardiac catheter in order to perform the angioplasty, the builder's blood vessel, which had been nearly completely blocked, was now only 30 percent blocked. There was now no need for angioplasty or open-heart surgery.

Today, six years later, the builder meditates twice a day, practices aerobic exercise five days a week, maintains an ideal body weight by keeping his fat and sugar intake low, and is enjoying a life that has been literally rejuvenated.

Based on thousands of personal experiences like these, it is clear to me that the future of medical care lies not only in preventive medicine, but also in taking and finding integrative ways to treat illness—whether it's serious illness such as cancer and heart disease or less serious problems such as minor back pain.

In 1977, this was radical thinking. Now, of course, we know that exercise, nutrition, and stress management are the three treatments of choice for most cases of coronary artery disease. They're also the tools you can use to extend your life—and to make the years you gain healthy, enjoyable years. But back then, I felt alone in my conviction that the future of medicine and health care in the United States was prevention, not cures.

## A career in prevention

Luckily I found a much-needed guide in Dr. George Sheehan, a cardiologist who, at age 50, discovered that he could run his way back into good physical condition. He gave me help and encouragement as I explored new ground, learning lessons that were to have a profound impact. I was also fortunate to spend time with Dr. Kenneth Cooper, author of *The Aerobics Way*, one of the original texts on the value of exercise, and founder of The Cooper Aerobics Institute in Texas.

Thanks to the influence of these two men, and the lessons that I was beginning to learn about the healing properties of the mind-body connection taught in Eastern healing philosophies, I was able to look beyond what had been my horizons and envision my career in an entirely new way. I took a leave of absence from my practice to teach patients about nutrition, exercise, meditation, and the proper use of supplements. By 1981, I decided to leave surgery forever.

My new career in integrative medicine began in earnest when I was recruited to begin rehabilitation programs for a large hospital district in South Florida. My current practice in Boca Raton uses many different methods, including

Ayurvedic medicine, acupuncture, and homeopathy, as well as cardiac rehabilitation, stress management, and counseling to help patients take control of all aspects of their health. Ayurvedic medicine is the oldest form of natural medicine. It utilizes the principles of keeping the body healthy through sound nutrition, yoga exercises, meditation, and staying in spiritual balance. Food and herbs are the only medications used.

Thousands of patients have gone through my cardiac rehabilitation program. They've given me overwhelming evidence that regular exercise improves health. But the most important and rewarding part of my practice is teaching that, while our years may add up, with fitness, good nutrition, vitamin and mineral supplements, and meditation, we can control and even prevent the illnesses that lead to debilitation—the real enemy.

## Your own path to health

Do you have to become a vegetarian, compete in triathlons, or even jog every day in order to lead a long, healthy life? Not at all! But you do have to find your own way to exercise, and your own way to create healthy diet and lifestyle.

You can do it. Just as I changed and overcame obstacles, so can you. Just as I convinced myself that a life of good health for 126 years is possible, you can do the same.

In the chapters that follow, I will teach you seven simple techniques that you can use to change your life.

As a former hard-driving, overweight, sedentary smoker who found health, vitality, and happiness, I can testify from personal experience that these techniques really work. And it's easy to get from here to there.

## Fighting Cancer With Prayer

A young man, 27 years old, came to me with multiple brain tumors (*glioblastoma multiforme*). While he had already undergone radiation and chemotherapy, there was no operation that could remove all his tumors. He had recently married, his wife was pregnant, and he had a strong desire to live long enough to see his first child.

I started him on some of the Ayurvedic herbs that I use to bolster the body's own immune system and changed him to a vegetarian diet. I also taught him a type of meditation, which he performed for 20 minutes twice a day, and a form of mental imagery that would help him decrease the size of his tumors. After six months, much to the astonishment of his chemotherapy and radiation physicians, a repeat MRI of his brain showed that his tumors had completely disappeared.

Not only did this young man see his daughter being born, he began a new life. During one of his meditations, he had a revelation that part of the reason for the onset of his disease was the way he had lived his life—full of anger, drinking heavily, and even abusing his wife. He regained his belief in God, prayed daily, and recognized that from that point forward, his sole purpose was to do good in the world. The result was the development of a unique hospital program. Every time new patients were diagnosed with cancer, his organization was called to talk to the patients about the hope offered by alternative medicine and about things they could do to improve their lives and survive their disease.

He was thriving, he was enjoying his daughter, and his wife thought she had found an entirely new husband—all of which he attributes to being reconnected to his Creator. There is no question in his mind that the Ayurvedic herbs and meditation had given him the ability to re-establish his relationship with a higher power. He also believed (and I agree) that the many prayers from his community and church had helped his tumors disappear.

A lot has been written about the healing power of prayer in the last several years, especially by Larry Dossi, M.D., author of *Healing Words* and *A Prayer is Good Medicine*. Though I may not be able to convince you that this is the main reason my patient's tumors disappeared, I can tell you that he was tumor-free until his untimely death several years later. He had a fatal seizure, which the pathologist attributed to a tumor that had invaded his spinal cord. But the pathologist was wrong. There was absolutely no evidence of tumors in any part of his body at the time of his death. In reality, he died as the result of a complication caused by a drug that a neurologist had kept him on even after his recovery—a drug that he never should have been on to begin with.

You already have the tools you need:

• Your mind—and your willingness to meditate, to train yourself, to eat properly, and to pray.

• Your body—and your commitment to a complete exercise program, including aerobics, stretching, and weight training.

• Your diet—and your decision to lower your total caloric intake, reduce sugar and simple carbohydrates, eliminate toxic chemicals from your food, and use organically grown fruits and vegetables.

• Your search for alternatives to invasive medicine—and your growing understanding of how to use antioxidants, herbs, and other forms of natural medicine to maintain perfect health.

• Your spiritual quest—and your discovery of who you are in the universe and your relationship to Nature and to a higher power.

So—if you're ready—now is the time to follow me and start your journey toward healthy longevity.

## My Own Brush With Surgery

Although I've been practicing medicine for 30 years, I continue to learn more and more about the mind-body connection. While one of the first things I discovered is that physical exercise is essential for good health, there is an even more important component.

Over the course of the last nine years, I have discovered the unknown healing factor within the human body. I call it the Apollo Factor, for the Greek God Apollo. In Greek mythology, Apollo passed his powers of healing on to his son Asclepius, who became the god of healing. Within each of us, the Apollo factor is the power to effect spontaneous healing.

When stimulated by positive messages, the Apollo Factor affects the body at the cellular level and makes changes that fight cancer cells, reverse heart disease, lower blood pressure, and prevent the onset of disease to begin with. Whether you believe in God or Nature or a universal consciousness, we know that the universe was created with a higher level of energy than any one of us has individually—and that the energy of the universe remains constant. By connecting with this higher level of energy, no matter what name you give it, you stimulate the Apollo Factor within you.

I've often said that if I had my arm cut off, I'd want to be taken to the best surgeon that could be found—but if I have an illness of any kind, take me to my Qi Gong master. Well, in 1998, I was taken to the hospital because I had a funny feeling in my body.

This feeling was initially diagnosed as a heart attack—but I knew that there was no way this could have been a heart attack. There were no changes in the enzymes in my heart muscles, and there were no changes on my electrocardiogram. Still, I was being told that I needed a cardiac catheterization. I said, "NO." The cardiologist insisted, and told my wife that without a catheterization, he could not guarantee that I would survive. My response was, "No catheterization. No angioplasty. No open-heart surgery. This is not a heart attack."

This was understandably frustrating for my cardiologist, Dr. Seth Baum. But since he believed that a patient has the right to participate in his own care, he agreed to abide by my wishes. I was put in the intensive care unit, where I raised eyebrows by requesting to have Master Fu, a Chinese Qi Gong master, come to evaluate me that evening. I had learned Qi Gong exercises from Master Fu, and also had studied acupuncture under him. I wanted him to assess the energy system of my body through Chinese pulse diagnosis to see if he agreed with me that this was not a heart problem that I was experiencing, but something far less serious.

Most of the nurses who had finished their shifts waited to find out what Master Fu was going to do. Much to their surprise, he walked in, waved his hands over my body as I lay there hooked up to monitors, put his hand on my pulse, put his hand on my chest, looked at me and said, "Your heart is fine. The problem is with your lungs. You have too much chi in your lungs. You need to come to see me when you finish in this hospital."

To satisfy my cardiologist—and to make sure there really was no cardiac problem—I underwent an electrocardiogram. It was normal. I underwent a thallium stress test. It was normal. My cardiologist finally agreed that I could be discharged from the hospital, but insisted on sticking to his diagnosis that I'd had a "minor heart attack." I knew, though, that I'd really had some sort of blockage of chi caused by overstressing my lungs. And that once the chi was cleared, I would be fine.

I immediately started acupuncture treatments with Master Fu, and over the course of the next six weeks, the chi cleared considerably and I was back to being able to exercise on a regular basis.

Here's the rest of the story—proof that healing occurs when we do those things that bring us back to health (i.e., stimulate the Apollo Factor): In 1999, I competed with my wife and our 22-year-old son in a Hi-Tech Adventure race—a six-mile run through the woods, combined with an hour and a half of kayaking, combined with a 12-mile mountain-bike course. Between those events, we had to climb a 12-foot wall carrying buckets of sand, crawl under cargo nets, run through mud, and deal with many other "obstacles" that were put in our way. I repeated the event in June 2000, this time with my 23-year-old and 35-year-old sons. My wife, Donna Lee, is now a competitive ballroom dancer. I am still an adventure racer!

Back in 1984, I completed what I thought would be an impossible task—to complete the IRONMAN Triathlon in Kona, Hawaii. Today, that is once more my dream.

# CHAPTER 2

# SMASHING THE AGE BARRIER

◆

*I'm going to open a door for you. On the other side of that door, you'll find all the tools you'll need to lead a healthy and vital life for 100 years or even longer. Tools that will enable you to change your whole life and the way you live it—to make your heart, lungs, and muscles stronger, to strip fat from your body and replace it with muscle, to free yourself from back pain, to manage stress in your life, and to enjoy a vibrant sex life no matter what your age.*

*You'll also find the tools you need to actually ward off the effects of aging, protect yourself against heart attack, stroke, cancer, and other illnesses—and even reverse many disease processes.*

◆

Before you read any further—before you learn in any more detail about my program to health at age 100—I want you to think about how long you want to live and what quality of life you wish to enjoy.

Say you're 30 years old and you want to live to be 120 years old in good health—to spend your last day driving a fancy sports car to pick up a hot date. That's a realizable goal.

Say you're already 70 years old. You want to live as long as you can and, at the same time, you want to undo damage done by decades of smoking and eating too much fat-laden food. That, too, is possible.

Or, perhaps you're like I was not too many years ago. You're in your mid-30s, stressed out from overwork, overweight from too many burgers and fries, out-of-shape, and not very happy. And maybe (as I did) you want to add years to your life, feel better, and find a more satisfying way to spend your days. I know it's possible. I did it!

As a society, we need to realize that good health and vitality up to and past the age of 100 is possible—for us. We know that it's possible for other people, because we hear about them all the time.

Centenarians (people who are 100 years old or older) are the fastest-growing segment of our population. The second-fastest group is people who are 80 or older. Currently, there are about 50,000 centenarians in this country—a little more than one for every 10,000 Americans.

Prior to the 20th century, the average life expectancy was about 45 years of age. However, it's important to distinguish between "average life expectancy" and lifespan. Average life expectancy is the average age to which members of a population survive. Lifespan is the maximum age obtainable for the species, and is defined by the age of the oldest living individual. In the case of humans, that individual was Jeanne Calment, who died at the age of 122 in August 1997.

There are many other examples. Shigechiyo Isumi, a Japanese fisherman, lived almost 121 years. Bellong Mahathera, a Cambodian monk who started a new life as a Buddhist leader in the United States at the age of 90, lived to the age of 110. And today as you're reading this book, it's quite plausible that yet another person is breaking the longevity records.

People who live to be 100 are big news in our culture. We read about them in our local papers. We hear about them on morning television. We congratulate them and applaud them.

But why do we applaud? Merely because they've lived to be 100? And if so, what does that say about our views on aging and about how long we expect to live ourselves?

It says, I believe, that most of us expect to die long before we reach 100, because we think there is something extraordinary about anybody who lives to be 100. We think this way even though there is no biological reason why we can't all live to be 100 years old or older.

## Quality of life versus quantity of years

If you believe that adding years to your life means adding years in which deterioration, pain, and illness are unavoidable, years you're likely to spend in a hospital bed, you might wonder why you'd ever want to live to be 100 or older. If you believe that extending your life for an extra 20 years means no more than giving up wellness in exchange for an extra two decades of painful inactivity, chances are you'd opt for fewer years.

I know that if the certainty of death and decline were all I could expect from extending my life, I'd have to say I wasn't interested.

But I expect to live to 126 years old. That's the target age I've set for myself. And I want those "extra" years to be not just a decade or two "tacked on" to the end of my life. I want them to be years that are free from pain and illness and gradual decay. I want them to be filled with happy experiences and growth and activity.

Just as it's true that you can live past 100, it's also true that growing older does not have to mean growing into a life of pain and feebleness and decreasing vitality. Just as research points the way to a life span that extends far beyond the average live expectancy of 75 years, it also tells us how to fill our lives with vitality, vibrancy, and health.

Just plain common sense tells me that many other Americans share my desire for an active, healthy life decades beyond the average life expectancy. There's also statistical evidence that proves that most people don't just want years added to the end of their lives. They want years filled with health and vitality.

One survey, for example, commissioned by *Parade Magazine*, showed that 66 percent of 2,503 respondents said the thing they feared most about growing old was living beyond an age where they could care for themselves and maintain good health.

## How old are you really?

Here's a medical fact: Chronological age has little to do with biological age. You've probably made this observation yourself without recognizing how it applies to your own life. For example, do you know a 40-year-old who looks and acts 10 or even 20 years older? Have you ever met a 70-year-old who looks and acts like 40 or 50? And don't we all know a few ageless, indefatigable old-timers who, like the Mississippi River, just keep rolling along, year after year, seeming somehow to grow younger though their chronological ages creep higher and higher?

Your biological age, not your chronological age, determines how long you live and the quality of the life you live, in terms of health and well-being. And so it is your biological age that should be of the utmost concern to you. What's your biological age? It's a measurement of health that is calculated on how strong your heart and lungs are. The most accurate determination of biological age is to measure the body's ability to consume oxygen during an exercise test. This measurement is known as V02 max. The higher it is, the younger your biological age. Most of us achieve our highest VO2 max at age 22. During the aging process, this number usually falls by 1 to 5% a year. So you can see that a 70-year-old whose VO2 max is still the same as the average 40-year-old is biologically 40 and chronologically 70. Blood tests for DHEA (Dehydroepiandrosterone) and IGF1 (Insulin Growth Factor 1) fall as we age. Normal DHEA for a 20-year-old male could be 450–700 mg/dl, while normal IGF1 for the same person is 800. By the age of 80, IGF1 is less than 100. So, again, an 80 year old with a high DHEA and high IGF1 are biologically younger than their chronological age.

The bad news is that you can do nothing about your chronological age. The good news is that biological aging can be slowed. In fact, in many cases biological aging can be stopped. And in some cases, it can be reversed. We have overwhelming scientific evidence that this is possible.

Consider, for example, the effects of exercise. Fred Kasch, who, at age 80, is the head of the Exercise Physiology Lab at San Diego State University, tracked the results of exercise on a group of 12 men for a remarkable 28 years (the longest duration of any such study I know of).

One of the men in the study has not gained a pound in 30 years. He has the same blood pressure he had three decades ago, and has the aerobic power (the heart and lung capacity) of a 25-year-old, even though he's a

61-year-old grandfather.

Another participant in the long-term study has better aerobic power (defined by Kasch as the ability of the heart and lungs to deliver oxygen to the body's blood and muscles) at age 75 than he did when he first started exercising at age 47.

What all the scientific research and anecdotal evidence tells me, beyond any doubt, is that you don't have to look forward to growing "old" at 50 and spending the rest of your life dealing with the illness and disease and helplessness that have for generations been associated with the aging process in America.

This means, for example, that an overweight, out-of-shape, 35-year-old male who smokes, drinks, and lives under stress, and who, therefore, has a biological age of 60 or older, can follow the regimen outlined in this book and quickly reduce his biological age to 50, and then to 45, and then to 40, and even to 35 or 30. The fact is that anyone can reduce his or her biological age by following my program.

That's right. You have control—in fact, a great deal of control—over just how you age. You don't have to simply sit back and allow your body to deteriorate. You can stop some of the aging processes before they get started. You can inhibit, and even reverse, others that may already have started in your body.

## Who are the Centenarians?

Dr. Kenneth Pelletier, Ph.D., author of *Longevity: Fulfilling Our Biological Potential*, says that such cases of long life are "not unique . . . [and that] instances of healthy longevity of 90 to 120 years have been documented in

many other societies since at least the sixth century B.C."
To back his claims, Dr. Pelletier cites instances of healthy
longevity which have occurred in the Andes and in Pak-
istan. These instances, he concludes, "are an indication of
a biological potential [to live long, healthy lives] inherent
to the human species as a whole."

Dr. Pelletier also points out Socrates, the Greek philosopher, who, it is said, lived for 98 years; Heraclitus of Eph-
esus, another philosopher, who lived for 96; Pythagoras,
the philosopher mathematician, who reportedly died at age
91; and Michelangelo, who painted the Sistine Chapel and
wrote poetry until the time of his death at 89. More recently, Bertrand Russell (yet another philosopher) lived to be
98. Bernard Shaw, the philosopherdramatist, lived to be 94.
Pablo Picasso, the painter, lived to be 92. And playwright
George Abbot, at the age of 100, brought a revival of his
first hit, "Pal Joey," to Broadway.

A 1995 research report from the Office of the Vice
President for Research at the University of Georgia
showed that most people who pass their hundredth birthday live independently (or semi-independently), are active
in their communities, and enjoy relatively good physical
and mental health (compared to people in their 60s). For
example, at 104, Mary Sims Eliot was working on her
autobiography, writing poetry, and trying to influence her
church position on social issues. She is currently 105, and
her autobiography, *My First 100 Years*, was just published.

At 105, Geneva McDaniel taught aerobics daily at her
senior citizen center. Now she's 107, and still recruiting
residents of her retirement community to exercise with
her. At 106, former sharecropper Jesse Champion and his
86-year-old wife Fronnie continued to weed and harvest
their own garden. Recently, Fronnie passed away, and

## HOW AGE REDUCTION WORKS

# How Young Do You Want To Be?

You can reset you own biological age. Just how much time you add to your life and what kind of time you enjoy depends on two factors:

1. Your age when you begin to take control of your own health and your own life, and,

2. How far you're willing to go to implement changes in your life.

Let's look at these two points in a bit more detail.

How old are you now? How long you live and the quality of life you enjoy depends, to a great extent, on how old or young you are when you begin to take control of your own health. That's just common sense. As much as I'd like to believe that there's a program out there that will guarantee 120 years of life to everybody, that's not the case. A 70-year-old with a history of heart disease who follows my program cannot expect the same results as a 30-year-old athlete who implements the seven steps.

The 70-year-old will, however, add years to his or her life. Just as important, he or she will feel better and stronger and will have less pain and more vitality.

Think of the 70-year-old and the 30-year-old as two automobiles. One is a two-year-old sports model with 10,000 miles on its odometer. The other is a classic with 100,000 miles under its belt. The first car is showing just a few signs of wear, while the second is rattling a bit, has bald tires, and needs shocks.

Wouldn't a program of regular preventive maintenance and repair benefit both autos? You bet it would!

But since the first car started its program in near-new condition, it might be expected to continue running in good shape
for 200,000 or even 300,000 miles. The second car's results
might not be so striking, but it would be reasonable to expect
it to run in much better shape for many more miles than
would have been the case without any regular upkeep and
maintenance.

The simple fact is that my program is, in some important
ways, exactly like a repair and maintenance program for an
automobile.

Secondly, how far are you willing to go to implement
change? Just as an automobile maintenance program requires
the exercise of discipline and effort, so does a program that's
guaranteed to keep you alive and healthy longer. Why? Because just as it does a car limited good to burn high-test gasoline if its spark plugs are dirty, so it does your body limited
good to eat a diet rich in cancer-fighting nutrients while you're
smoking a pack a day of non-filtered cigarettes.

You are the one who will determine, to a huge extent, how
long you will live. You will also determine the very quality of
your life—how much freedom from pain you will have, how
active and alert you'll be at age 40, 50, 90, and beyond, how
much sex you'll be able to enjoy now and later, and how much
vitality you'll be able to bring to all your activities. If a longer,
healthier life—a life that finds you still healthy at 100—is
your goal, the time to start achieving that goal is today, no
matter what your age.

The important thing to remember is that it is never too late
or too early to begin putting my program to work. It can truly
add years to your life, whether you are an out-of-shape 65-
year-old or a 23-year-old athlete. And you'll start to reap the
benefits almost immediately.

Jesse, now 107, lives and gardens with his daughter.

I'm not saying life will be limitless. Aging is natural and inevitable. Death is natural and inevitable. What is neither natural nor inevitable, however, is feebleness and sickness and pain at 50 or 60, and death at 75 or 80.

But experts say elderly survivors are focused on the here and now, not the hereafter. They are just as active in mind as in body. As Mary Sims Eliot put it, "I'm too busy to die."

Successful aging has many components. Heredity is not as important as you would think. As one expert points out, people are not likely to live a long time just because their parents did. It seems that genetic contribution is important in some centenarians, but not all of them.

Centenarians are found in all walks of life. Some have doctorate degrees and some have little or no formal education. Some are affluent and some are so poor they lack even the necessities. Most of them, however, have a wealth of family and friends or they rely on their wits to build a strong support network, which is one of the main factors in living a long, productive life.

The govermental researchers were surprised to find very little depression among centenarians. They are highly self-sufficient and are confident and resourceful in their ability to overcome obstacles. In general, they describe themselves as "I-can-do" people.

About 50 percent of the centenarians in the study try to avoid fats in their diets, and almost all of them include more fruits and vegetables in their diets than their younger counterparts. Sixty percent rate their health as "good to excellent," and an even higher percentage say it is "as good or better than it was five years ago." David, a gentleman mentioned in the University of Georgia report is 105. He has 20/25 vision and still reads without glasses.

And Julia, a 100-year-old retired seamstress, still threads her own needles.

Centenarians have an incredible ability to cope with hardship and loss. They are also very spiritual, and have a deep trust in God. They believe that everyone should have his own philosophy of life, but don't believe in imposing theirs on other people. For the most part, they have a great deal of wisdom, and feel that their lives have made sense. They also think that even at the age of 100, people have the ability to change some things.

## Three basic principles

The seven steps outlined in this book will help you do three things: repair the damage that's already been done to your body; prevent further damage from occurring; and help you dodge the bullets that can prevent you from living healthily into your second century. These bullets are the debilitating and deadly illnesses that most of us wrongly assume are the necessary baggage of middle and old age.

I view any death before age 100 as an early death. How can I possibly say this when most people die long before they reach 100? Easily. Because most people do not die of old age. They die of disease or accident.

Now, we can't control accidents. In fact, living fully may expose us to more risk of them than we would be subject to if we stayed in our homes and never did anything exciting like bicycle riding or mountain hiking—or bodysurfing or skydiving.

But as long ago as 1938, a senior pathologist in Great Britain reported in the medical journal *Lancet* that never, in his long professional career, had he performed an autopsy on an individual who died of old age. All the cadavers he'd had on his table had died of disease.

More recently, researcher S. J. Olshansky of the University of Chicago's Department of Medicine went high-tech and presented a scenario—based on a computer model—in which the average life expectancy of humans would approach 100.

Olshansky forecast average life expectancy gains that would be realized if high-risk, illness-causing lifestyle choices (smoking and improper diet, for example) were eliminated, and if the killer diseases cancer, heart disease, and diabetes were removed as causes of mortality. His research, reported in the November 2, 1990 edition of the journal *Science*, showed that, given those circumstances, the average life expectancy for both men and women would leap to about 99.2 years.

These killer diseases are the bullets you'll have to dodge to live into your second century. And you can reduce your risk of most of them by taking the steps outlined in this book.

But you'll not only reduce or eliminate such risk factors. You can reverse damage that has already occurred. While it's true that people who begin living healthfully at a younger age can make more gains, all the studies I've mentioned, coupled with anecdotal evidence and experiences I had in my years of medical practice, taught me that anyone can add healthy, vital, energetic years to his or her life span.

For example, the most remarkable demonstration I've ever come across of the power of simple exercise to reverse the aging process involved 10 residents in a Boston nursing home who were instructed to lift weights three times weekly, for 10 to 20 minutes each time. Within just eight weeks, these residents—who ranged in age from 86 to 96—had more than doubled their strength. Even more exciting, two of the 10 had tossed away their canes and were able to walk unassisted for the first time in years. And one man had risen, without help, from a chair that had held him captive. Keep in mind that these were elderly people who were described by Tufts University researcher Maria Fiatarone as "people who are about as sedentary as human beings can possibly be, and almost as old as any human being can be."

By implementing these seven steps, you'll also prevent future damage. To use exercise as an example again, abundant evidence proves that it wards off disease. Researchers at the Stanford University School of Medicine in Palo Alto, California looked at the health habits of 10,269 Harvard University alumni over an eight-year period. They found that moderately active men—men who took part in such sports as jogging, swimming, and running—had a 23 percent lower risk of dying from any cause than men who never worked out. Another long-term study performed at the University of California at Berkeley followed 10,000 Harvard graduates 45 to 84 years old. It showed that men who take up moderately vigorous forms of exercise such as tennis, swimming, jogging, or brisk walking reduce their overall death rates by as much as 29 percent. And they have a 41 percent lower risk of coronary artery disease than men who don't exercise.

Yet another study, sponsored by the Institute for Aerobics Research in Dallas, Texas, followed more than 10,000 men and 3,000 women for an average of more than eight years. The researchers found that those in the study who exercised had lower death rates from all causes—as well as lower reported rates of colon cancer, coronary heart disease, hypertension, and stroke.

## The seven steps to vital living

I'm convinced that it's possible to actually have a biological age (an age measured by your overall health, your
heart strength, your lung capacity, your muscle tone and
mass, and your bone mass, among other things) far below
your actual chronological age.

I'm sure Mavis Lindgren from the little town of Orleans,
California, would agree. Mavis—at age 80—regularly runs
26-mile marathon races.

So would Lucille Thompson of Danville, Illinois. Lucille, at age 88, was troubled by arthritis and decided to
take karate lessons in an effort to ease her pain and increase mobility. Two years later, at age 90, the 4'11" great-
grandmother was awarded her black belt and the unlikely
nickname "Killer."

Just as it is possible for "Killer" Thompson in her karate
dojo to live a healthy life far longer than most of us ever
thought possible, you, too, can enjoy health, vitality, mental sharpness, and freedom from pain far longer than you
ever thought you could.

The seven steps that will help you do it are:

1. Self-Assessment: Taking the measure of your health
   and your risks
2. Aerobic Exercise: Keeping your heart and lungs
   young
3. Supplements and Antioxidants: The secret to
   dodging disease
4. Stress Reduction: A benefit for mind and body
5. Strength Training: Working muscles to banish aging
6. Flexibility Exercises: Betting on your back and joints
7. Healthful diet: Changes to make for a lifetime

## The single best thing you can do to live longer

Here's the most powerful longevity secret of all. If you want to live to be 90 or 100 or 110, what you must do, starting right now, is think you can.

That's right, just thinking, and eventually believing, that you will live a long life sets in motion a series of other thoughts and actions that—cumulatively—will help you live longer. Unless you're 100 already, or just about to celebrate your 100th birthday, this belief just by itself should have a powerful impact on your life.

For example, if you're 40, you have ahead of you the near-equivalent of what you once believed was a full life— another 60 years or more. And if you're 50, you have another 50 years of life to enjoy, maybe even 60 or 70.

When, in this scenario, does so-called "middle age" begin? Not at 40, surely. Not even at 50. If you're 65, you're not a "senior citizen," no matter how many discount cards you carry. Senior citizens are in their 80s or 90s.

So, if you're 40 and have decided your chosen line of work doesn't make you happy, you have plenty of time to go back to school and prepare yourself for a second career. If you always wanted to learn to play the accordion and never quite had time, now you do. If your spouse passes away when you're 65, you have the option of building a new, long-term relationship.

## Accept a new way of thinking

No matter how old you are now, you have a chance to live a longer, healthier, and more vibrant life than at any other time in the history of humanity. But to do this, you must start by believing the evidence that a longer life is yours for the taking.

Turn your back on the belief that life is a 75-year journey from youth to old age, from wellness to illness, from vitality to feebleness—and that on this journey you must adhere to some sort of degenerative timetable that gives you just so much healthy time and no more.

Turn your back on the belief, so prevalent in this society, that productive life ends when you reach the mandatory retirement age of 65. Or, at the latest, when you blow out the candles on your 75th birthday cake.

Turn your back on the belief that it's normal, even expected, that your body will wear out as you grow older. That by the time you're in your 40s, the old machinery will be starting to show signs of wear and tear. Your knees will creak, your belly sag, your arteries harden, and your bones soften.

And turn your back on the idea that diseases like heart disease and cancer and diabetes and Alzheimer's are an unavoidable part of the aging process.

Why? Because turning your back on these ideas robs them of their strength. Accepting a new way of thinking—namely, that you will live a long and healthy and vibrant life—sets in motion a process that ultimately invests you with the strength you need to make that thought a reality.

I know that you have the will to embrace these ideas. I've told you how I came to embrace them in Chapter 1. I'll ask you to make a promise to yourself in Chapter 3.

# THE COMMITMENT TO CHANGE

◆

*Right now—before you read any further into this book, before I tell you about all of the seven steps, before I open that door to greater vitality and longevity for you—I want you to make a simple, yet unconditional, commitment.*

*I want you to make a contract with yourself to do your best to exercise according to my "Rule of 3s." You'll promise to read Chapter 5 and take part in some sort of aerobic exercise or sport for 30 to 60 minutes, three times a week, for three months.*

*That's all.*

◆

You don't have to promise to become a world-class athlete. Nor must you train yourself to run a five-minute or six-minute mile. But you must do your best, your very best, to do some sort of aerobic exercise for 30 to 60 minutes, every other day, for a three-month period.

The exercise you choose can be as simple as taking a walk in the park. Or you can jog or work out on a rowing machine. Do whatever you enjoy and whatever is comfortable.

Sounds simple, right?

It is.

But without this commitment, you may as well put down this book right now. Because your sense of responsibility for your own health is the foundation upon which all your future gains will be built. Without this commitment, success will be less likely.

## The importance of commitment

My own experience of changing from an overweight, overworked, out-of-shape wreck into a healthy, happy man capable of competing in triathlons taught me just how important commitment is. It also taught me that it's necessary to take one step at a time to put that commitment to work.

If you remember, I did not change overnight. My change started when—urged by a friend to enter a three-mile race—I realized how terribly out-of-shape I was, and I decided to begin running. Other changes followed. I started a program of weight training to go along with my aerobic exercise. I made changes in my diet that included my decision to become an ovo-lacto vegetarian. I began practicing meditation and stress reduction techniques. And, most recently, I began using dietary supplements to give my body added protection against disease and aging.

My own commitment to change was easy once I realized that, by not changing, I was putting my life in jeopardy. I first had to admit that I'd lost control over my own health. Then I was able to accept the fact that, unless I took action, I was headed for serious health problems and an early death.

I have to assume that you've already accepted the idea that you need to make some changes in your life, or you wouldn't have read this far in a book that's all about change. And I'm hoping that you accept—in your gut, not just in your mind—the fact that you are the one who is responsible for these changes. Because it's all up to you. Unless you take action, nothing will happen.

It has been my experience over the past 20 years of practicing alternative medicine that the most important change to make, initially, is to begin to feel better by becoming more physically fit. Every one of my patients who has accepted this has taken dramatic strides forward. If you underestimate the importance of making this first step, if you fail to commit to exercise aerobically at least 30 minutes a day, three days a week, for three consecutive months, the rest of this book will be far less effective for you.

If you are already exercising—if you have already made and are continuing to keep this commitment—you should make a commitment to make one of the other six steps a part of your new healthier lifestyle. If I had to choose just one step, my choice would be meditation, because I believe that it is in the stillness of the meditative state that we gain knowledge of the universal consciousness and what is good for us as individuals. The meditative state allows us to tap into the Apollo factor. It is also in the stillness of meditation that your body, especially the central nervous system, is rejuvenated. The central nervous system drives all the organs of the body. When this system is healthy, the mind and body function synergistically.

So you could make a commitment to attend a meditation class and to meditate for 20 minutes twice a day. Or you could make a commitment to change your diet and lower your cholesterol. Or, if you're worried about bone density or feel tired and weak, you might make a commitment to increase your muscular strength by lifting weights three times a week for three months. You might join a yoga or tai chi class and make a commitment to do that three times a week for three months.

## Don't look back on your life with regret

One of the heirs to the J. Paul Getty fortune said, when he was in his 80s and close to death, that he regretted that he had spent his whole life making money. He was sad, he said, that he'd never taken the time to use his money in any meaningful way. He'd never traveled for the fun of it—had never taken the time to learn anything other than what he needed for business. He said he was terrified, as his death approached, that his last words were going to be, "I wish I had taken the time to . . . ."

The same basic sentiments are expressed by an anonymous poet who wrote:

*If I had my life to live over, I would relax more*
*I wouldn't take so many things so seriously*
*I would take more chances*
*I would climb more mountains*
*I would swim more rivers*
*I would ride more merry-go-rounds*
*I would pick more daisies*
*The next time, I'd start going barefoot earlier in the*
   *spring and stay that way later in the fall*
*I would not make such good grades in school unless I*
   *really wanted to*
*I would relax more.*

I find the words of both the anonymous poet and the Getty heir to be profoundly moving. It is bad enough that they both speak with such sorrow about opportunities lost. What is worse, at least in my mind, is that their words indicate an acceptance of the status quo. They have simply given up and accepted the idea that they can't change the course of their lives.

Oh, I know you can't relive your past and make it different any more than I can recapture the time I lost when my whole life was centered around my career. You can, though, learn from your past.

You can look back at your life, take stock of what you've done, and say to yourself, "Okay, I've made mistakes. I haven't taken charge of my own life. I haven't stopped to smell the roses. I haven't taken care of myself. But now I'm going to change. I'm going to be the master of my own fate. I'm going to do things differently!"

## Close the door on the past

I ask you—urge you—to close the door on your past the way you'd close the door on a room you never want to see again. You really can't do anything about what you did (or didn't do) yesterday. Instead, open the door to the future and start living your new life: a life in which your past mistakes and shortcomings play no role except to serve as lessons on what not to do.

Immediately after I ran in my first three-mile race, I decided to shut the door on my past and move on to a new, healthier life. I didn't want to find myself 80 years old and in poor health, bemoaning the fact that I hadn't climbed any mountains or taken the time to walk barefoot in the surf. To make sure that I didn't end up like the anonymous poet, I immediately opened the door to a new way of life.

## Just get started

My experience tells me that you, too, will find change

easier than you imagine once you finally get started. And you get started by making the commitment I asked you to make at the beginning of this chapter. By making a contract with yourself to do some sort of aerobic exercise for 30 to 60 minutes, three times a week, for three months. When you make this commitment, you will be accomplishing two major goals.

1. You will be admitting you need to change.
2. You will be taking the all-important first step to realizing that change.

If, at first, you're unable to live up to your contract—if, for example, you exercise for just two weeks and then give up—that's okay. Start over again, at any time, so long as the end result is three consecutive months of aerobic exercise. The purpose of this commitment is to enable you to see the benefits that accrue from making even a minor change to a more healthy lifestyle change.

Why commit to exercise before any other step? Because we're all the products of an impatient society, a society in which we've been taught to expect instant gratification. Aerobic exercise is the fastest and simplest way I know of for you to begin to change yourself. I know—I guarantee—that almost as soon as you start to exercise, you'll lower your body fat and you'll feel better. And when you look in the mirror, you'll see results!

## What exercise should I choose?

While there are many kinds of aerobic exercise, at this point you should consider putting walking or jogging at the top of your list. I recommend these activities in the beginning because you can do them without joining a gym or a health club and without spending a lot of money on equipment. These are also activities that most people find enjoyable.

Actually, a brisk walk is not only the easiest way to start a program of aerobic exercise, it's also one of the most efficient. Many people have reported that walking—around the neighborhood or around an air-conditioned mall—led to changes in physical condition and feelings of health and well-being that exceeded their wildest expectations.

Later, perhaps, you might decide to buy an exercise machine—a StairMaster, an exercise bicycle, a NordicTrack, a treadmill, or any of the other aerobic machines that are currently available. But for now, choose an activity that doesn't involve a big expense.

## You can find the time

You may think you can't possibly fit three exercise sessions each week into your already overcrowded, busy schedule. But you can. I have many patients who are busy executives or single parents. Inevitably, the first time I talk to them about exercising three times a week for 30 minutes or more, they swear they can't possibly fit exercise into their busy schedules. But once we look carefully at the way they spend their time, we're able to fit in the exercise.

The first step is to make sure you pick an activity you like. I know from my own experience and from my work with my patients that you will find a way to make the time to do something pleasurable. In fact, I know that once you start a form of exercise you truly enjoy, you'll quickly reach a point where you wouldn't miss one of your thrice-weekly sessions for anything.

Next, sit down with a pad of paper and a pen and write

out a schedule showing your daily activities over the course of a typical week. Then examine your schedule and see what you can do to free up some time.

Maybe you watch the morning news for 30 minutes before you leave for work, and then the evening news for 60 minutes after you return home. Cut out one or the other three times a week, and exercise instead. If you feel information deprived, put on headphones and listen to radio news while you work out.

Perhaps you take an hour for lunch every day. Take a

## Keeping and Renewing Commitments

It will only take this moment of your time to make a commitment to exercise. Keeping that commitment is a different story. The first happens in an instant; the second is an ongoing journey.

Though I have exercised continuously since 1975, there have been times when it was difficult to maintain my commitment. From late 1997 to early 1998, for example, I fell out of my regular routine. I tried to go to the gym and work out with weights. I tried to get on the treadmill. I tried to ride my bike outdoors. But frankly, I was bored with the entire exercise process.

So I went back to the basic principle that has always worked for me. That is, I made a commitment.

I found a personal trainer by the name of Carl Bousquet, a former competitive bodybuilder. I committed to work with him at least three days a week short lunch every other day, and spend the time you save walking or jogging.

Be creative. Take a quick shower instead of a long, lazy tub bath. Skip a situation comedy that you usually watch—or tape it and watch it another time. Consider cutting back on your work hours.

Schedule your exercise sessions the same way you schedule appointments or meetings. What you're doing here, after all, is finding the time to add healthy years to your life.

for a period of three months, paying for the first twenty sessions in advance. The three months expanded to five months, and the number of days I worked out with Carl increased from three to five. He relentlessly pushed me to my limits. This effort, and Carl's encouragement, gave me back the feeling of accomplishment I had experienced in the past during the times I trained for marathons, triathlons, and the Ironman competition. I had lost that triumphant feeling because I didn't have any goals to shoot for.

By the end of that five-month period with Carl, I had lost 20 to 25 pounds, and was as physically fit from a muscular point of view as I was when I played football at Boston College. Best of all, I was back on track.

What I learned from my experience is that commitment is ongoing. You have to keep refreshing your goals, creating new ones when the old ones have been reached. And the ultimate goal is to live in the present—not in the past, and not in the future. Simply take it one day at a time, doing the best you can on your goals each day.

By shifting activities, I found the time to run from six to 10 miles, five times a week, when I was working 20-hour days as a cardiac surgeon. To be sure, it took some ingenuity on my part. I did paperwork on my coffee breaks and I read in the bathtub.

I'm sure you have the same kind of ingenuity. Even if you work a back-breaking 12 hours a day, seven days a

## Seven Ways To Squeeze In Exercise Time

Here are some more ways you can find the time you need to exercise:

• Prioritize, prioritize, prioritize. When you analyze your daily or weekly schedule, you'll find small sacrifices you can make for the sake of exercise. Perhaps you can go to sleep a little earlier at night, so you can wake up a little earlier in the morning. Or perhaps you can take a commuter train instead of driving your car, so you can work or do reading on your way to and from the office.

• Schedule real "power lunches." These are two-hour breaks away from the office when you can exercise and eat a healthy lunch. Taking care of your health is real power.

• Consider exercising before you go home from work as a regular extension of your workday. You may find it easier and more efficient to exercise before you go home to shower, eat dinner, and relax.

• Ditch the car. Walk or ride a bike to the store when you run errands, or walk to work if you live close enough. I rode a bike to and from my office, about 10 miles a day, five days a week, when I trained for my week, and sleep for eight hours a day, you still have four hours a day (28 hours a week) for other activities. Out of that 28 hours, you only need a maximum of three hours a week for your aerobic exercise schedule. If you're serious about your health, you'll do what you have to do and find that time.

first Ironman Triathlon. When I drive to work now, I pass one fellow who walks to work every day. In the last eight weeks, I've seen this man's body go through some amazing changes. I've literally seen pounds melt off his frame. If you take public transportation to work, consider walking instead—at least one way. Or, get on and off at a stop that's a mile away, and walk the extra distance.

• Think like a child. Find ways to work in exercise that feels like play. For example, as many of my readers know, I am an avid Harley enthusiast. When I have to bring my motorcycle in for repairs, instead of finding someone to give me a lift, I use this as an excuse to play. I take my Rollerblades along in a backpack and rollerblade the five miles home. Then, when it's time to pick up the motorcycle, I put on my running shoes and enjoy a five-mile jog to the repair shop.

• Use the weekends. If you're really strapped for time, make use of Saturday and Sunday. Since you don't need a cool-down day between aerobic sessions like you do with weight training, you can exercise two days in a row. If you exercise on Saturday and Sunday, you'll have to find only one more hour for exercise during your busy work week.

## Take one step at a time

Once you've made your commitment to exercise for at least 30 minutes a day, three times a week, for three months, be wary of committing to any other changes, at least in the beginning.

Why wait? In my experience, many men and women who are serious about making important health changes can become almost compulsive. They want to change everything immediately. If you try to do this, you're bound to fail—particularly if you haven't paid any attention to your health for years.

I am not saying that you shouldn't be excited at the prospect of good health. I hope that you're chomping at the bit, ready to leap into this program and break all speed records for becoming healthy. However, in the beginning, it is important to take one thing at a time. Don't try to change everything all at once.

Keep in mind that this is a long-range program, and it may take you several years before you have made aerobic exercise a habit in your life. Recognize that it takes at least nine months (and sometimes as long as 18 months) to create a new habit.

The best path to success is to wait until you have moved at least part way along one path before you make another major change. Only you will know when you are ready to take the next step. I can't give you solid rules on how quickly to proceed. Once you start a program of aerobics, for example, it may take you a full year or more to become a habitual exerciser. You may be comfortable doing aerobics plus practicing some formal method of stress management after just a few weeks or months. However, you may want to wait a year before moving on.

(Incidentally, just doing the aerobic exercise will help relieve some stress.)

It is up to you. You have the freedom to move at your own pace. You should feel no guilt if it takes you three or four or even five years to become completely habituated to your new way of life. The important thing is to keep at it.

I know you want to achieve perfect health today. That you want to put the entire program for healthy longevity to work right now. But I urge you to be patient. My experience with my own life and with patients in my Florida clinic has shown me over and over again that slow and steady progress, over time, is a better and more certain path to ultimate success.

Later in this book, I'll talk specifically about exercises—aerobics, weight training, and flexibility—that you can use to strengthen your heart, lungs, bones, and muscles and loosen your joints, about stress-reduction techniques (including meditation), and about ways that you can change your diet to lose weight and feel great without feeling hungry all the time. For now, though, remember to be gentle and patient with yourself as you begin to modify your life.

## Exercise, health, and happiness

I know from experience that as soon as you get started on a more physically active lifestyle, you'll be better able to cope with the stresses of everyday life. Your self-esteem will be enhanced. You'll be more content in your work. You'll be more creative and productive.

Skeptical? One of the "typical" and seemingly unavoidable symptoms of aging is loss of memory and a lessening

## Beating Negative Thinking

Don't let yourself be trapped into failing in your commitment by believing that you can't succeed. Below are some things to remember to help you smash these negative thoughts whenever they occur to you.

• "I'm too old to start." No matter how old you are, you're not too old to be physically active. There's no such thing as being too old to begin some sort of exercise program.

• "My family was fat. I'm doomed to be fat." You're not doomed by heredity to be overweight. No one has to be overweight unless he or she chooses to be overweight.

• "My life is out of control. How can I control my health?" There's no reason for your life to be out of control. But recognize that you are the only one who can take charge. When you accept that responsibility and begin to change the areas in your life that need change, you'll be well on your way to a happier, healthier, and ultimately longer life.

• "I only worked out one day last week. I should just give up." This is the worst type of negative thought. No one is perfect, and creating new habits isn't easy for anyone. There's no shame in failing to put in your three days—as long as you're willing to pick yourself up the next week and start again. If you fail, at least you know you were in the race.

As a friend of mine once said after the two of us finished last in a 6.2-mile race, "Think of all the people sitting at home who can't even think about running 6.2 miles!"

of the ability to solve problems. This loss supposedly begins occurring early in life.

But researchers at the University of Kentucky reported that people who do aerobic exercise boost their ability to recall names and perform other mental tasks. These findings mirror those of a University of Maryland study that showed that fit older men and women are better at solving math problems than older people who don't exercise.

I'm a firm believer that after three months of aerobic exercise, three times per week, for at least 30 minutes, you'll be more satisfied and happy with your life as a whole. And being more positive will help you continue to believe in yourself, and believe in your ability to stay healthy, which will help you to continually renew this commitment and eventually add all seven steps to a longer, healthy life.

Ayurvedic physicians often say, "If you want to know the status of the mind a year ago, look at the body today." In other words, your thoughts, your motivation, your spirituality, and your consciousness have as much to do with your health as anything that I might teach you. If you can keep this first commitment for a full year, your body will reward your resolve in ways that will astonish you.

I'm so sure of it that I'm including a contract for you to sign. It's one way to make your commitment to better health concrete and visible.

Evidence that you can actually slow or even stop the aging process and enjoy additional years of active, vital life far beyond your 60th or 75th birthday is all around us. This evidence has convinced me that there is, in fact, a way for you to add years, maybe even decades, to your life while enjoying good health and well-being that until now you may have associated only with youth.

Consider, for example, Vanacha Temur, whose story was told by Dr. Deepak Chopra, in his book *Ageless Body, Timeless Mind*. Vanacha—a native of Abkhasia, a mountain region in southern Russia—who claimed an age of 110, was visited by a group of American journalists. They found that the old man was spry, alert, and full of life and vitality.

> "Vanacha's vigor . . . was incredible. A man of about five feet with twinkling blue eyes and an elegant white mustache, he was the personification of a kindly and playful grandfather. He credited his slim, wiry body to light eating, horseback riding, farming, and walking in the mountains."

The old fellow had in his possession a baptismal certificate that showed he was 106 years old. But, he explained, his parents had waited four years to baptize him, while they saved money to pay the priest.

Whether he was 106 or 110, Vanacha, with blood pressure of 120/84, was a remarkable example of healthy longevity. He was not, however, atypical—at least not in his own society. According to Dr. Chopra, a study of Abkhasians aged more than 90 showed that fully 85 percent were mentally healthy and outgoing, only one in 10 had poor eyesight, and only 4 percent had poor hearing.

Such anecdotal evidence that healthy living even at age 100 and beyond is possible has been amassed with increasing regularity in recent years. It has been amassed with enough regularity that we can no longer look at Vanacha and others who live healthy lives for 100 years as freaks who somehow beat the odds—as exceptions to the rule that life ends at about age 75.

## Your Commitment To Health

I, _____ (name), hereby commit to exercise aerobically at least three times per week, for a minimum of 30 minutes, for at least three months, beginning today, _____ (date). I promise myself to think only positive thoughts about my exercise program. I promise to begin counting weeks at the beginning if I skip two or more sessions in a row, or skip one session for two consecutive weeks. I promise not to give up, even if I do have to start over. I promise to focus only on this new commitment until I have fulfilled it, and to then evaluate what I must do to continue fulfilling it. I promise to use my creativity to find the time for this commitment. And I promise to make it fun!

Most of all, I promise to exercise mindfully, noticing and enjoying the changes that occur in my body and attitude. I promise to be patient and gentle with myself, remembering that nothing happens without a beginning. And I promise to exercise safely, consulting my physician or other practitioner before I begin, especially if I have any current health conditions or am taking any prescription medication.

Signed,

AGEproofing

# CHAPTER 4

# ASSESSING YOUR RISKS

◆

*According to my wife, Donna Lee, the trick to living a healthy life at 100 is: "Do not croak before your hundredth birthday." However, there's more to it than that.*

*When I was in my early thirties, I discovered that the average heart surgeon (which is what I was at the time) died by the age of 54. You can imagine the surprise and fear that overtook me. Then I found out that conductors of music often lived, productively, well into their nineties and beyond. It fascinated me that those who knew about the body died prematurely, while those who knew about the sounds of music lived for such a long time.*

◆

I found that Albert Einstein, who had mastered the quantum energy theory of nature, also had great insight into the energy theories of health. In a letter to a friend in 1954, Einstein said, "To one bent on age, death will come as a release. I feel this quite strongly now that I have grown old myself and have come to regard death like an old debt, at long last to be discharged. Still, instinctively one does everything possible to delay this last fulfillment."

We all die prematurely. So, of course we want to do

"everything possible to delay this last fulfillment." If all our body parts were well-maintained, we could live at least 120 years in good health. (That's why the 20 questions I'm about to ask you could save your life.)

In my youth, I thought life was a game. So I played too much, too long, and too hard. Soon I found that my body would not permit me to to go on in this way. When I was too zealous in athletics, my injuries increased.

I became aware of the fact that some of the best athletes in the world develop disease prematurely. Muhammad Ali developed Parkinson's disease when he was still a young man. Joe Namath, one of the best football players to ever play in the NFL, can barely function on a golf course because of damage to the cartilage in his knees.

Though I knew that exercise is great medicine, I learned that excessive exercise is not. In time, I discovered that the best way to maintain a healthy body—even better than with exercise—is through meditation. It is the mind that determines the fate of all the cells of the body.

That is why musical conductors tend to live such long and healthy lives. They not only work at a job they enjoy, they actually work in a meditative state. A conductor becomes so absorbed by the musical vibrations emanating from his orchestra that he achieves an altered state of consciousness similar to that of the yogis of India who spend their lives in meditation. I'll tell you more about meditation in Chapter 7.

## A long, healthy life is your choice

If you're like most people, you have not practiced alternative medicine as long as your children will. You didn't realize that good health is your choice. Instead, you were brought up to believe that doctors are in charge of your well-being. Now you know that the choices you make, the food you eat, and the state of your mind, soul, and body will determine how you live—and how you die.

At the age of 35, I decided that I wanted to be healthy at age 100 and beyond. I looked to physically active centenarians as my role models. I discovered that, on average, they are optimistic, they are happy, they are spiritual, they have a strong tolerance for adversity, they have close family and friends, and they do not suffer from chronic degenerative diseases such as arthritis, heart disease, or cancer. When they die, the cause is usually listed as "old age."

Connecting the mind and body is the secret. Physical longevity is the result.

## Beyond the physical markers of aging

According to the book *Biomarkers: The 10 Determinents of Aging You Can Control,* by William Evans, Ph.D., and Irwin H. Rosenberg, M.D., the biomarkers of aging are:

1. Your muscle mass
2. Your strength
3. Your basal metabolic rate
4. Your body-fat percentage
5. Your aerobic capacity
6. Your body's blood-sugar tolerance
7. The ratio of your total blood cholesterol to your level of high-density lipoprotein (HDL)
8. Your blood pressure
9. Your bone density
10. Your body's ability to regulate its internal temperature

Though the book makes some very strong points about aerobic capacity, blood-sugar tolerance, body fat, and strength and muscle mass, it deals only with the physical factors of aging. Certainly hormones play a role. So do heredity and lifestyle.

However, a healthy life at 100 goes beyond the physical. It is an attitude. It is an intention. It is the mind—and I do not mean the brain—directing the physical body into healthful habits that will allow you to be productive and happy at the age of 100 and beyond.

In other words, you can't focus all your attention on your body and ignore the psycho-neuro-immunologic effects of your mind.

That mind and body connection forms the foundation of the 20 questions in this chapter, questions that I have developed over the course of my years as a doctor. These 20 questions will help you learn what changes you need to make to prolong your life well beyond your hundredth year.

**Question #1:** Are you a spiritual person?

## ☐ yes ☐ no

Webster defines the word "spiritual" as not only relating to the soul, but also as concerned with the refinement of thought and feeling that is associated with the intellect. Obviously, there are religious connotations to spirituality. But in this context, I am asking only whether you recognize that there is some sort of higher power—whether it be God, the natural power of the universe, or an unknown physical energy force—that controls not only our environment, but also our bodies. In other words, I'm asking you if you are aware of a higher power that has an effect on your health.

If you answered no: You'll want to pay special attention to Chapter 7.

**Question #2:** Do you meditate, pray, or spend 15 or 20 minutes of quiet time daily with imagery, self-hypnosis, biofeedback, relaxation therapy—or any other natural means to raise your awareness to a higher level of consciousness?

## ❏ yes ❏ no

In this question, I'm asking whether you take time for yourself and use a specific technique (especially meditation or centering prayer) that allows you to rejuvenate your central nervous system. It doesn't include going for a walk or golfing, although both of those activities can be relaxing.

We know that people who meditate generally have lower blood pressure, lower blood sugar, less heart disease, and fewer incidences of cancer. When they develop an illness, they spend fewer days in the hospital and often resolve their health problems more rapidly. And they deal with others in a much kinder way.

In my opinion, quiet time, prayer or meditation, practiced for 20 to 30 minutes before your day begins and at the end of your work day, is powerful medicine. And it's absolutely necessary for longevity.

If you answered no: You'll want to pay special attention to Chapter 7.

**Question #3:** Do you have solid, nurturing relationships?

## ☐ yes ☐ no

This question is designed to see whether you have developed support groups–not only within your family, but with friends and people of like interests. If you are religious, for example, this means you not only go to Sunday or Saturday or Friday night services, you also participate in those services with a group of people on whom you could rely for help if you ever need it.

Good, close connections with others definitely prolong healthy life. For example, one of my patients who is well into her seventies has, as one of her support groups, a class of children who need help in learning how to read. She teaches those children three days a week. This activity has had such a positive influence on her health that she has reduced her cholesterol from an abnormal high of 300 milligrams per deciliter to about 190 milligrams per deciliter. And her cholesterol had been elevated for thirty years!

**Question #4:** Are you happy?

## ☐ yes ☐ no

Are you content with your job? With your relationships with other people? With your relationship to the universe? When you wake up in the morning, do you say something like, "I feel great! Thank you for allowing me to be here for another day?"

Happiness, no matter how you define it, is a very, very important factor in healthy longevity. Norman Cousins, who was once the publisher of *The Saturday Evening Post*, might have said that happiness has to do with laughter. His first book, *Anatomy of an Illness*, was written about his personal experience in curing himself with humor. Later in his life, he taught at UCLA Medical Center where his book, *Head First: The Biology of Hope and the Healing Power of the Human Spirit*, was used as a textbook for medical students.

In my practice, I have found that those who are content with the way they have lived their lives—not necessarily with their accomplishments—are often the happiest.

If you answered no: You'll want to pay special attention to Chapter 7.

**Question #5:** Do you have hobbies?

## ☐ yes ☐ no

One person's hobby may not seem like much fun to someone else. Your hobby may be reading. It may be writing music. It may be playing the guitar or piano. Or creating figures out of wood. It may be macramé, knitting a sweater, or making a quilt. A hobby is any activity that you enjoy and that also creates a balance between the mind and the body.

People with hobbies tend to be more content with their lives. So if you don't do anything except work, eat, exercise, and go to church, my advice to you is to develop some outside interests. Hobbies should be fun but not necessarily physical, unless you're like me and love physical work. Gardening or learning a new computer program is just as important as taking part in a bicycle or swimming club. The goal is to be interested in a lot of things.

If you answered no: You'll want to pay special attention to the resource list below.

## Choosing a Hobby

Consider your choice of hobby as a way to play a game, by yourself or with others. Do not consider it as another job. Here are some ways to find an enjoyable hobby that brings both relaxation and social connection into your life.

• Attend adult education classes that focus on activities you've always wanted to try. Once you've learned the basics, see if there isn't a club in your area that lets you practice or improve your skills in the company of other people.

• Check out your community's senior center or recreation center. They'll often have classes, activities, and travel programs.

• Attend church or synagogue functions—not just services. Your house of worship probably has choirs, instrumental groups, or dramatic programs. And it probably needs adults to sponsor or chaperone youth trips.

• Try gardening, photography, cooking, painting, or creative writing.

• Join a sports club. Whatever outdoor activity is popular in your area, it's likely that there's a club for your age group that offers classes, matches, or competitive events.

• If you have trouble finding the activity you've selected in your area, search the Internet, or ask a local librarian to help you do so. You might also try scanning the "Clubs and Organizations" listing of your local newspaper.

**Question #6:** Do you enjoy restful sleep?

☐ yes ☐ no

By restful sleep, I mean that you go to bed at a reasonable hour, you get 6 to 8 hours of sleep (depending on your body type and your physical needs) and your sleep is not interrupted during the night. Ideally, you should go to bed between 9:30 and 10:30 p.m. and wake up (without an alarm clock) before the sun rises in the morning, feeling completely rejuvenated and full of energy.

Restful sleep (also called REM sleep) is a very important component of health and longevity. This is the period, usually about forty-five minutes a night, when growth hormones and melatonin are stimulated in the brain. When your sleep is interrupted, you do not produce growth hormone, which may be considered as the fountain of youth. If you deplete it, you grow old faster than expected. You need melatonin to have vitality, and it should be restored during sleep to relieve the stress of daily living. When melatonin is low, your physical body wears out.

If you answered no: You'll want to pay special attention to Chapters 7 (meditation) and 5 (aerobic exercise).

**Question #7:** Do you have regular bowel movements at least once every day?

## ❏ yes ❏ no

Ideally, healthy people eliminate once after each meal. It's the body's way of insuring that any toxins you may have ingested are excreted. You should have one to three regular, soft (not constipated) bowel movements every day. This is a sign that you are in good health, that you have good digestion, and that you are assimilating nutrients properly.

Constipation and diarrhea (loose, semi-formed or non-formed stools) are abnormal and are indicators of the risk of developing serious gastrointestinal illnesses.

If you answered no: You'll want to pay special attention to Chapters 10 (diet) and 5 (aerobic exercise).

**Question #8:** Do you have a good appetite?

**❑ yes ❑ no**

You should be hungry in the morning before breakfast, before lunch, and before dinner. This is an indicator of normal digestion, normal digestive enzymes, and good health. The lack of appetite is a sign of sluggish digestion and poor digestive enzymes.

On the other hand, if you are constantly hungry or have bouts of hunger between meals, you may have an abnormal fluctuation of hormones in your body, particularly the insulin levels that control blood sugars.

A lack of appetite can mean colon and rectal problems, and an overstimulated appetite often indicates small intestine and stomach problems. Both of these abnormal extremes can lead to gastrointestinal disease, gall bladder disease, and other liver dysfunctions, including pancreatic diseases.

If you answered no: You'll want to pay special attention to Chapters 10 (diet), 7 (meditation), and 5 (aerobic exercise).

**Question #9:** What is your energy level? On a rating scale of 1 to 10, with 1 being no energy and 10 being boundless, childlike energy, is your energy level at least a 7?

**❑ yes ❑ no**

If you don't feel up to engaging in activities you enjoy, you can't call yourself healthy. Energy level is affected by whether you have good cardiovascular health, an adequate flow of oxygen to the tissues, good elimination of toxins, and fully functioning organs, including the organs that develop red blood cells and control brain hormones and chemistry.

People with low energy levels may have a physical ailment. Low energy levels are also associated with psychological, neurological, or immune-system problems, and with disorders that involve all three of those dimensions. Disorders of the nerves and of brain hormones can lead to low energy levels; so can psychological diseases such as bipolar disorder, depression, and schizophrenia.

A lack of energy is one of the earliest manifestations of the onset of heart disease, chronic fatigue syndrome, low (hypo) thyroid function, inadequate adrenal function, diabetes, and high blood pressure.

If you answered no: ALL chapters of this book may be important for you. Because low energy levels can have a physical cause, your best bet is to see a holistic medical practitioner to rule out any existing disease. Then you should most likely take ALL seven steps to age-proof your life. Your energy levels will most likely normalize—and you'll add years to your life.

**Question #10:** Do you exercise aerobically on a regular basis?

## ❒ yes ❒ no

Aerobic activity helps maintain good oxygen flow to all

of the body's tissues and helps prevent the onset of high blood pressure. It is estimated that if you were to exercise for just 30 minutes, three days a week, you would reduce your risk of death from heart disease by as much as 50 percent. In fact, if you already have developed heart disease—even if you have never exercised before in your life—you should consider aerobics to be the most important medication you have. (But if you do have heart disease, you should consult your doctor before beginning an exercise program. He or she will likely be thrilled!)

Ideally, you should be doing some form of sustained exercise that elevates your heart rate to an individually calculated training level for a specific number of minutes.

If you answered no: You should pay special attention to Chapter 5 (aerobic exercise).

**Question #11:** Do you do flexibility and strength training, yoga, or tai chi a minimum of three days a week?

## ❏ yes ❏ no

Longevity is prolonged by flexibility and strength training as much as it is by aerobic activity. While some might disagree, I believe that the orthopedic limitations of aging lead to more deaths in people over the age of 70 than any single chronic disease. When joints are stiff and bones are brittle, exercise is difficult, coordination deteriorates, and accidents from falls are more likely.

Therefore, you should be doing musculo-skeletal training (weight lifting), tai chi, or yoga (I recommend the Sun Salutation, a sequence of specific poses) on a regular basis. A minimum is three times a week for 10 to 15 minutes.

If you answered no: See Chapters 8 (strength) and 9 (flexibility).

**Question #12:** Is your body fat percentage ideal?

❐ **yes** ❐ **no**

The ideal proportion of body fat to total body mass for a man is 16 percent; for a woman, it's 20 to 22 percent. You can have your body fat measured in three ways—by impedance, by underwater weighing, or by a skin-fold measurement. Underwater weighing is the most accurate way to find your ideal weight, which is a very important element in insuring healthy longevity. You can estimate your ideal weight by remembering how much you weighed between the ages of 18 and 22 (assuming you were muscular and physically fit at the time).

But it's definitely worthwhile to have your body-fat percentage tested at a local gym, fitness center, or senior center.

If you answered no: See Chapters 5 (aerobics), 9 (flexibility), 8 (strength), and 10 (diet).

**Question #13:** Are you on a calorie-restricted diet?

❐ **yes** ❐ **no**

Evidence shows that the neo-paleolithic diet, a lean diet that is low in simple sugars and high-glycemic foods such as white rice, potatoes, pasta, bread, and alcohol, prolongs life. This means you should eat three to four whole fruits per day and three to four cooked vegetables per day, and simply skip the empty starches. While I prefer protein predominantly from vegetable sources such as beans, brown rice, and soy products, you might prefer animal protein. It's a fine source, as long as the animals were fed balanced, hormone-free diets. The manner in which the animals were treated will be a factor in your health.

Pure water (a minimum of ten glasses per day) is an ideal nutrient. You can also drink antioxidant-packed green tea. Avoid alcoholic, sugared, or artificially sweetened beverages. Keeping your body hydrated helps it circulate nutrients and keeps it flushing toxins through sweat and excretion.

If you answered no: See Chapter 10 (diet).

**Question #14:** Do you consume more than five alcoholic beverages a week?

## ❐ yes ❐ no

I believe that alcohol should be restricted to no more than five alcoholic beverages per week. Many experts believe that no alcohol should be the rule of thumb. However, because there is evidence that there is some protective effect from the flavonoids in red wine, I condone the consumption of up to five glasses of red wine per week.

But that doesn't mean two glasses of red wine per day—and it certainly doesn't mean beer or hard liquor.

Meanwhile, if you want to avoid alcohol altogether, you can get those bioflavonoids in supplement form (they're discussed more fully in Chapter 6).

**Question #15:** Are you smoke-free—meaning you do not smoke now and have never smoked cigarettes?

☐ **yes** ☐ **no**

If you have smoked in the past, you should be without cigarettes for a minimum of one year for every year that you smoked. Obviously, if you smoke now, you have to quit smoking. (And that includes cigars and pipes, even if you do not inhale them.)

If you answered no: See Chapter 6 (antioxidants).

**Question #16:** Do you have essential fats in your diet?

☐ **yes** ☐ **no**

Your body requires essential fats for balanced nutition. You must take in omega-3 and omega-6 fatty acids in order to maintain the health of your cells and immune system. Essential fats also are critical in the prevention of degenerative diseases of the brain such as Alzheimer's, schizophrenia, and chronic depression.

My recommendation is a minimum of 1,000 milligrams of omega-3 and 1,000 milligrams of omega-6 fatty acids daily. I consider these the two most important fatty acids. These fats can be obtained from cod liver oil capsules, EPA (eicosapentaenoic acid) capsules, borage seed oil, evening primrose oil, flaxseeds, or flaxseed oil. I recommend combining either cod liver oil or EPA with flax, borage or evening primrose.

If you answered no: See Chapter 6 (antioxidants).

**Question # 17:** Do you take antioxidants daily?

☐ **yes** ☐ **no**

I agree with Dr. Denham Harmon's free-radical theory of aging. It explains that, no matter where we live, we all are in a toxic environment because free radicals are constantly attacking our body's systems. The antioxidant chapter discusses these compounds in more detail, but in the simplest terms, their existence means that we are all rusting internally. And that means we have to take antioxidants daily to help counteract the damage.

If you answered no: See chapter 6 (antioxidants).

**Question #18:** Do you have one or more of the following diseases in your family history: coronary artery disease (not valvular disease), diabetes mellitus (also known as Type II or adult-onset diabetes), high blood pressure, or cancer?

## ❐ yes ❐ no

Because these major degenerative diseases have a small genetic link, people who are predisposed to develop them should pay very careful attention to their answers to Questions 1 through 17, and they should do so all of their lives.

For example, a 20-year-old whose father died of a heart attack at the age of 55 should never, ever smoke cigarettes, because smoking will drastically increase his risk of developing heart disease.

Some practitioners might argue that high cholesterol should be on this list. However, I do not believe that high cholesterol, in and of itself, is a major risk factor unless it is accompanied by a strong family history of heart disease. Diabetes, cancer, and high blood pressure play just as great a role in early death as does heart disease.

If you answered yes: You'll want to pay close attention to ALL of the chapters in this book. Many facets of health have an effect on these degenerative diseases. You'll want to fight them in every way that you can.

**Question #19:** Even if the following diseases are not in your family history, do you have high blood pressure, cancer, atherosclerotic heart disease, diabetes mellitus, or stroke?

## ❏ yes ❏ no

These are the major oxidative, degenerative diseases. In order to live healthfully to age 100 and beyond, you must do everything possible to reverse these diseases.

If you answered yes: Pay close attention to ALL the recommendations in this book.

**Question #20:** Do you know your blood levels of the following: DHEA-S (DHEA sulphate), IGF-1 (insulin growth factor), fasting insulin level, free and bound testosterone, and cholesterol?

## ❏ yes ❏ no

You need to know these blood levels are the levels in order to determine your physiologic (not chronologic) age. Many people who have a chronologic age of 60 have a physiologic age closer to 90. So, because we're ultimately looking at a healthy lifespan as being 120, you need to pay attention to these blood levels and do something to supplement or change them if they are deficient.

The DHEA-S test is the simplest and most reliable indicator for both men and women in determining healthy age. I believe that by the age of 70, your DHEA-S levels should remain at least 100. A more reliable test for predicting physiologic age is the IGF-1 level, which begins to decline at age 20. Even at the age of 80, if you have an IGF-1 level of 140–150, you can expect a long, productive life.

Hormone analysis is also very important. First of all, your fasting levels of the hormone insulin should be less than 20. Excess insulin accelerates the aging process by affecting other hormones in the body and creating bad prostaglandins, cellular chemicals that can cause disease. (Good prostaglandins prevent disease.) Too much insulin also promotes early breakdown of tissue and excess body fat, eventually diabetes, and early death. So control insulin—one way is to reduce carbohydrate intake—and you remain healthy longer.

For women and men, estrogen and testosterone levels are important. If you're a woman, you should also know your progesterone level. I find that saliva tests levels of these hormones are more accurate than going by the levels obtained in blood tests.

In my opinion, there has been too much emphasis placed on cholesterol levels and not enough emphasis on the association of testosterone levels with heart disease. Cholesterol is on my list only because atherosclerosis and coronary artery disease in the United States are, to a certain degree, associated with abnormal cholesterol levels. I do not treat cholesterol levels in my patients over the age of 70 with medications of any kind. Once you have reached the age of 70, I don't think it matters if your cholesterol is above 200.

Early in my career, a clinician told me that ideal total cholesterol should be 100 plus your age. There is no need for you to look for a more sophisticated calculation than that, although your levels of HDL (the good cholesterol) and LDL (the bad cholesterol) should be taken into account.

Additional blood levels that are as important as cholesterol in determining the risk of coronary heart disease include fibrinogen (which determines clotting mechanisms), c-reactive protein (which is a determinent of the inflammatory nature of heart disease), homocysteine levels and lipoprotein A (LPa).

If you answered no: Your first stop—before implementing the life changes described in this book—should be your doctor's office. The tests you take there will help you focus on what health issues to tackle first. They might even save your life.

**Bonus Question:** This extra question may be of more importance than any others I've asked. Excluding your job, do you make a daily contribution to humanity?

## ❐ yes ❐ no

My 30 years of experience tells me that the answer to this question is critical in determining whether you will live a healthy, productive, happy life to age 100 and beyond.

As a physician, you might say that I make a contribution to humanity because I help the sick. Not true. If I want to stay healthy at 100, I have to reach out beyond that God-given talent. How I do it can be anything from working at my local church to serving food at a soup kitchen to coaching a Little League team. It can be providing shelter for the homeless, doing something to help protect the environment, or supporting a cause that works for world peace.

In all the people I have met throughout my life, I have found that those who live with the greatest vigor are those who give back to society.

## Your new resolutions

• Start every day by coming into balance with nature. Wake up before the sun rises by going to bed early and getting enough sleep.

• Release stress by meditating for a minimum of 20 minutes every day. Your meditation may include a mantra, a chant, a centering prayer, or any other practice that allows you to bring cohesiveness to your mind/body.

• Fine-tune your nutrition. Eliminate sugar from your diet, maintain your ideal body fat percentage, stick to a calorie-restricted diet, maintain the weight you were at when you were 18 to 22 years old, reduce alcohol, and drink pure water and antioxidant teas.

• Take omega 3 and omega 6 essential fatty acids on a daily basis.

• Supplement your diet with a minimum of the antioxidant vitamins A, C, E, beta-carotene and selenium, and with B-complex. Also consider coenzyme Q10, garlic, and shiitake mushrooms.

• Exercise for a minimum of 30 minutes aerobically, three times a week, and for 10 to 15 minutes with flexibility or strength training, tai chi, or yoga.

• Develop strong relationships.

• Follow the good example of five-year-olds: Laugh, play, and enjoy life. Take naps.

• Never hold a grudge.

• Make a contribution to humanity.

• Thank God every day for your existence.

CHAPTER 5

# AEROBICS

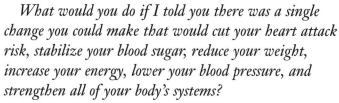

*What would you do if I told you there was a single change you could make that would cut your heart attack risk, stabilize your blood sugar, reduce your weight, increase your energy, lower your blood pressure, and strengthen all of your body's systems?*

*Surely you'd want to make that change, wouldn't you? At the very least, you would give it a fair trial to see if it was really the miracle cure that it promised to be.*

*That miracle is aerobic exercise. And it really can do everything I've just promised you.*

## Striving for maximum benefits

In 1981, Dr. George Sheehan, the author of *Running and Being* (Second Wind, 1998), wrote: "To Bob Willix—the surgeon who will eventually prove the knife is our lesser weapon. Exercise is the new medicine." In addition to being an author, Sheehan was a cardiologist and a philosopher.

Study after study has shown the benefits of aerobic exercise. That's why it's such an important part of my program—the first commitment that I ask you to make to improve your overall health.

As soon as you start to exercise aerobically, you'll almost

immediately begin to look better and younger, and you'll feel more vibrant and alive. If you continue exercising and fulfill your commitment, you'll feel even more benefits. But don't take my word for it. Take a look at the research for yourself.

## Even moderate exercise makes a difference

Recent studies show that an inactive lifestyle—too many hours spent as a couch potato and too few hours engaged in even simple exercise—contributes to about 250,000 deaths annually. People who don't exercise are twice as likely to suffer from heart disease as men and women who do exercise.

At the University of Utah Medical School, researchers found that regular participation in activities such as walking, bowling, raking leaves, and ballroom dancing was enough to reduce the risk of heart attack by 30 percent. And the University of Wisconsin Medical School proved that heart attack patients who took part in a specially designed exercise program were able to reduce their death rate from coronary artery disease by 25 percent—about the same rate as could be achieved by drugs, but without any side effects.

There are literally hundreds of scientific studies showing that aerobic exercise boosts your health. Aerobic exercise has been shown to reduce the need for insulin in adult-onset diabetics, to lower blood pressure in people with hypertension, and to reduce the risk of stroke. Researchers have also found that it decreases the deadly complications of Alzheimer's disease. Additional benefits include increased muscular strength, a reduction in bone loss from osteoporosis, and increased joint mobility in arthritis.

There is even a study indicating that exercising aerobically is one of the best ways for women to reduce the incidence of breast cancer.

And that's not all. Exercise also reduces anxiety, relieves some of the complications of stress and tension, and gives a boost to the body's immune system. There is no way not to look at exercise as the medicine of the future.

By taking my challenge—by living up to your commitment to my "Rule of 3s"—you will find in yourself a new balance between mind, body, and spirit. You'll be so satisfied with the results after just three months that I know you'll never go back to a life that doesn't include aerobic exercise for a healthy heart and longevity.

## Reverse the symptoms of "old age"

If you feel the strain on your heart and lungs whenever you exert yourself, don't think that this is a symptom of aging that you simply have to live with. Aging is not the problem. The problem is that you have allowed your body to become less efficient at obtaining the oxygen you need to produce energy.

Fortunately, this is a process that can be easily reversed with aerobic exercise. It can be reversed even if you've already started down the path to poor fitness. Even if you've moved far down the path.

Fred Kasch at San Diego State University documented how a 61-year-old grandfather had the aerobic power (the ability of the body to get oxygen and oxygen-rich blood to all its organs) of a 25-year-old. He also documented a 75-year-old who had better heart-lung capacity after taking part in Kasch's program than he did when he was 45.

Results like these are commonplace. And they can be

yours—will be yours—provided you're willing to under-
take a simple program of aerobic exercise.

## So what IS aerobic exercise?

I define as aerobic any activity that uses the large muscle

### Ken's Story

Ken was a busy executive. Overweight and out-of-
shape, he was too busy to take care of himself. At the
age of 32, he had chest pains—and, ultimately, four
heart bypasses. I met him when he was 36 years old
and looking for a way to reduce the risk of having to
undergo open heart surgery yet again.

Ken had never liked exercise. He had not been an
athlete as a child or as a young man, always preferring
to work with computers. But, as soon as Ken started
the aerobics program I set up for him, he noticed dramatic results. Within just three months, his weight
dropped from 232 pounds to 218, and he had more energy than he'd ever dreamed possible. Two years later, I
set out to convince him to run in a 5-kilometer (3.1
mile) race.

At first, he was skeptical. "I could never do that," he
said. "I've never run more than a few blocks in my life."

Finally, after a great deal of cajoling on my part, he
agreed—and, after a few more months of aerobic
training, I ran by his side in his first 5-kilometer race.
By that time, he'd been running four days a week for
three months and was down to 192 pounds. He was
thrilled by the cheers of the crowd along the race

groups of the body (for example, the legs in cycling and running, or the arms in swimming) in a rhythmic fashion. The thing that makes this kind of activity aerobic is that it gives the heart and lungs the ability to deliver enough oxygen throughout the body to keep us from going into oxygen debt.

course, by the attention of the media, and most of all by the proud looks he got from his wife and daughter when he crossed the finish line. He had proved not only what the average person is capable of doing, but also that a person with heart disease is capable of becoming above average. Keep in mind that he did this after having had open-heart surgery.

There's an interesting footnote to this story. After Ken ran his first 5-kilometer race in the early 1990s, he lost his desire to do any sort of physical activity. Then, in 1997, he went into a program sponsored by Dean Ornish—a vegetarian diet high in complex carbohydrates and low in fat. Despite this diet, Ken's triglycerides soared above 1,000. His weight went back up to more than 230 pounds—and because he had lost his aerobic capacity, he subsequently had another cardiac event and it was necessary for him to undergo another open-heart procedure that year. This convinced Ken that he had to stay aerobically fit. He now works with a personal trainer four days a week. He has regained his fitness and his health—despite two open-heart surgeries.

Remember, the commitment to change requires the commitment to continue—no matter how difficult it may be.

What is oxygen debt, and why is it bad? Oxygen is your body's fuel. Essentially, oxygen is to your body what gasoline is to an automobile. Stated as simply as possible, your lungs draw oxygen in, and your heart delivers that oxygen supply to every cell in your body, where it is used to create energy. The more efficient your heart is at delivering oxygen to your body's cells, the more oxygen your body has at its disposal, and the more energy you will have.

When the heart delivers more oxygen to your cells, your body can do more work with less effort. When you do aerobic exercise, not only does your heart learn to work more efficiently, it gets stronger. And you will have less of a chance of developing any illness, because exercise boosts your immune system.

## Become a student of your own heart

Chances are you don't know what kind of shape your heart is in. I can say that with a fair degree of confidence because most Americans don't.

Amazing, isn't it? Especially amazing when you consider that heart attacks will kill close to 1 million American men and women this year. And yet it's true. The vast majority of people, including those who are 35 years old or older and already among those most likely to experience heart trouble have never had even a resting electrocardiogram (EKG), let alone any of the more meaningful heart tests. Most people have no idea how good or bad a job their hearts are doing.

Well, prepare yourself, for as you continue your journey along the path to good health at age 100, you're going to become an avid student of your own heart. Before you begin your exercise program, you'll find out how healthy your heart is and you'll continue to monitor your heart's performance with regular checks.

A simple measure of the heart's efficiency is found in the rate of the body's oxygen consumption in terms of milliliters (ml) per kilogram (kg) of body weight per minute. The average oxygen consumption for healthy women and men is about 35 to 40 ml/kg per minute, while the oxygen consumption of a world-class endurance athlete (a biathlon competitor or a cross-country skier) may be as high as 65 to 80 ml/kg per minute.

An athlete using 40 ml/kg per minute is working at only 47 to 60 percent of his or her maximum capacity. Therefore, because the athlete's heart is stronger and is able to move more oxygenated blood per beat, the heart rate of that athlete is much lower than the heart rate of the average person exerting the same effort. The athlete is able to run both faster and farther, using the same amount of oxygen as the average person, but expend 40 to 50 percent less energy.

## How healthy is your pump?

There are several ways to measure the health, or more precisely the efficiency, of your heart muscle.

I recommend a stress test to all my cardiac patients. It involves measuring the electrical activity of the heart during exercise, while it's under stress. While it is not required to have a stress test to start a walking program or get on a bicycle, I know of no better way to find out about any problems you may have with your heart or blood pressure.

The typical stress test is administered to a patient while he or she walks on a treadmill or pedals a stationary bike. More advanced tests are available. The PET (Positron

Emission Technology) scan and the thallium and cardiolite scans are high-tech diagnostic tools that give a computerized, color image of the rate of blood flow to the heart muscle during exercise. Such tests reveal in a very sophisticated way whether there has been any damage to the heart.

A positive stress test is not a reason to panic. By revealing an abnormal electrocardiogram during exercise, the test indicates that the blood flow to the heart muscle is impaired. But you don't need to rush to the operating room. As a doctor, a positive stress test tells me that an exercise program is mandatory for that particular patient, and that a repeat test should be carried out in the future.

While some people believe that stress tests are risky, under proper supervision they are perfectly safe. Less than one in every 10,000 individuals who undergoes a stress test has a complication associated with the test itself.

## What stress tests can tell you

Most often, stress tests, whatever their form, are used as diagnostic tools to detect early signs of heart disease. Some physicians, including myself and Dr. Kenneth Cooper of the Cooper Aerobics Institute in Dallas, Texas, use stress tests to measure an individual's oxygen consumption and level of physical fitness.

In our laboratory, I have often seen a young individual who is not in good physical shape get on a treadmill and perform at the level of a 60-year-old. I have also seen individuals whom I otherwise would not have suspected had heart problems experience irregular heartbeats while undergoing a stress test. In my opinion, and in the opinion of Dr. Cooper, who has performed more than 80,000 stress tests, this measurement is the benchmark for assessing an individual's level of physical conditioning. It also can be used to determine what a target heart rate should be for aerobic exercise.

A treadmill test is an extremely valuable tool—provided the test is conducted by a preventive medicine specialist who is willing to take the time to observe the person taking the test.

## Do you have to get a stress test?

Many people choose to skip stress tests before beginning an exercise program, believing they are too young and too healthy to need one, or that the cost of such testing is too high. Ultimately, as with all decisions about your health, the responsibility is yours.

However, if you fall into any of the following groups, I strongly urge and advise and caution you to get a stress test. If you see yourself in the categories below, you should consider a stress test a requirement, not an option.

- If you're a male over the age of 35 or a female over the age of 45 who is not physically fit. (This means you if you score "fair" or below on the 12-Minute Self-Test described below.)
- If your immediate family history includes any individual who had heart disease before the age of 60.
- If you now have high blood pressure or diabetes, or have ever had them.
- If you have smoked within the past 10 years, any amount at all, even one cigarette a day.
- If you have a known EKG abnormality or a history of any type of heart disease.
- If you have any history of chest pain, dizziness, or shortness of breath.

- If you have a family history of sudden death before the age of 40.

If you fall into one of the above categories, it does not mean you won't be able to exercise aerobically to strengthen your heart. It does mean that your course of exercise may have to be moderated if—and only if—your stress test indicates a problem. It means you may have to work with your doctor to find ways to exercise that are safe for you.

## The 12-Minute Test

While the "gold standard" of physical fitness testing is a stress test coupled with an oxygen consumption measurement, there is another way you can assess your level of conditioning—the 12-Minute Test.

Originally designed by Dr. Cooper, this test measures the distance you can walk, jog, or run in a dozen minutes, and gives a very accurate indication of your fitness level.

Quite simply, the 12-Minute Test measures your fitness by measuring your oxygen consumption. But it does so without fancy laboratory equipment and without the need to be hooked up to a machine. And it is remarkably accurate.

In 1985, I administered the 12-Minute Test to 250 subjects in Florida's Broward County school system. The results of these tests were then compared to results obtained by measuring oxygen consumption during treadmill tests under laboratory conditions. While I did not test all 250 of my subjects, I randomly selected a large portion of them to be re-tested on the treadmill. The results of the 12-Minute Test that I administered and the results of the laboratory treadmill test were within five percent of each other.

Here's how to do the 12-Minute Test. First, find or lay

out a course two miles long. If you live near a high school or college, you may be able to use one of their indoor or outdoor tracks. Or perhaps you have access to an indoor track at a large YMCA or other club. If not, simply use the odometer in your car to measure a two-mile course in your neighborhood. (It's best to use a track, because you'll need to measure exactly how much distance you'll cover in 12 minutes.)

Dress comfortably and wear a watch with a second hand or an analog display so you can accurately gauge your time. Now hit the course, running or walking, but cover as much of that two-mile distance as you can in 12 minutes.

If you're able to make it all the way to the end, congratulations! You're in great shape. However, it is not necessary to run the entire two miles. You can run until you get short of breath, then walk until your breath returns to normal or near normal, and then run again. Or you can walk. However, at the end of 12 minutes, you need to measure the exact distance you managed to cover. (If you used your car's odometer, you'll need to mark where you stopped, and then drive the course to that point again.)

Then, using the chart below, a variation of one published by Dr. Cooper in his book *The Aerobics Way*), determine your physical fitness as measured by how much ground you were able to cover in the 12 minutes.

## What your score means

If you score below "good," you fail the test. And if you fail, you've got a lot of company. Most people—75 percent or so—fail the 12-Minute Test the first time they take it.

But as soon as you begin to fulfill your exercise

commitment, you'll quickly move from a "poor" score up the scale to "good," "excellent," and ultimately "superior."

If, however, you are a male over 35 years of age or a female over the age of 45, and you score below the "fair" mark, please take a stress test before you begin exercising—just to be safe.

## Why testing is important

The 12-Minute Test will tell you more than how fit (or

### Gauging your 12-Minute Test Results
#### Men:

|          | Superior | Excellent |
|----------|----------|-----------|
| Under 20 | >1.87    | 1.73-1.86 |
| 20-29    | >1.77    | 1.65-1.76 |
| 30-39    | >1.70    | 1.57-1.69 |
| 40-49    | >1.66    | 1.54-1.65 |
| 50-59    | >1.59    | 1.45-1.58 |
| 60+      | >1.56    | 1.33-1.55 |

#### Women:

|          | Superior | Excellent |
|----------|----------|-----------|
| Under 20 | >1.52    | 1.44-1.51 |
| 20-29    | >1.46    | 1.35-1.45 |
| 30-39    | >1.40    | 1.30-1.39 |
| 40-49    | >1.35    | 1.25-1.34 |
| 50-59    | >1.31    | 1.19-1.30 |
| 60+      | >1.19    | 1.10-1.18 |

unfit) you are today. You should use it every eight weeks to show yourself the progress you are making as you put your exercise program to work. If you have been exercising on a regular basis and your results on this test do not improve, you should consult a professional to find out (a) if there is something wrong with your heart or lungs, or (b) if you are doing enough exercise at the right intensity. Don't automatically assume there's something wrong with you. The problem could very well be the type of exercise you're using.

You can take the 12-Minute Test whenever you wish, at

| Good | Fair | Poor |
|------|------|------|
| 1.57-1.72 | 1.38-1.56 | 1.30-1.37 |
| 1.50-1.64 | 1.32-1.49 | 1.22-1.31 |
| 1.46-1.56 | 1.31-1.45 | 1.18-1.30 |
| 1.40-1.53 | 1.25-1.39 | 1.14-1.24 |
| 1.31-1.44 | 1.17-1.30 | 1.03-1.16 |
| 1.21-1.32 | 1.03-1.20 | .87-1.02 |

| Good | Fair | Poor |
|------|------|------|
| 1.30-1.43 | 1.19-1.29 | 1.00-1.18 |
| 1.23-1.34 | 1.12-1.22 | .96-1.11 |
| 1.19-1.29 | 1.06-1.18 | .95-1.05 |
| 1.12-1.24 | .99-1.11 | .88-.98 |
| 1.06-1.18 | .94-1.05 | .84-.93 |
| .99-1.09 | .87-.98 | .78-.86 |

no cost, and without any high-tech equipment. However, do not use this test itself as your aerobic exercise program. Even when you're just starting out, you need to do more than 12 minutes daily. I want you to know exactly how much aerobic exercise I recommend, and I want you to be aware of the full "menu" of exercises that you can do. Some of them will probably surprise you.

## Planning your exercise program

Your goal, as you exercise, is to achieve the maximum aerobic effect without crossing the line into anaerobic exercise.

Aerobic exercise is any activity that uses the large muscles of the body in a rhythmic fashion so that they deliver the oxygen the body needs to function well. During anaerobic exercise, the intensity of the activity is so high that the heart is not able to deliver enough oxygen to meet the body's demands.

As a result, we suffer what is known as oxygen debt. When this happens, lactic acid builds up in the muscles and we become fatigued. Anaerobic exercise can also put undue strain on an unconditioned heart, putting your health at risk. Sports that involve intermittent high-intensity activity, such as basketball, tennis, racquetball, 100- to 400-yard sprinting, baseball, and football, are anaerobic.

If you're out of shape now, you need to do only aerobic exercises. These include walking, swimming, bicycling, skating, jogging or running, jumping rope, certain types of dance and jazzercise, cross-country skiing, and rowing in a boat or on a machine. Any anaerobic activity can be made aerobic if it is performed at a slower, more regular pace.

It's interesting to note that even professional, world-class athletes who earn their livings by participating in anaerobic sports also exercise aerobically. Many National Football League teams, for example, have developed jogging, dancing, or cycling programs for their players. These fitness experts recognize the value of aerobics to build endurance. In fact, the athletes that are in the best condition of all, as measured by the strength and efficiency of their hearts, are long distance runners, swimmers, ballet dancers, cyclists, and cross-country skiers.

## Focus on cardiovascular endurance first

One of the basic goals of cardiovascular conditioning is to lower your pulse rate. When your pulse rate goes down, your heart will get more rest and will have to work less hard than the heart of the average individual who is not physically conditioned. For example, most long-distance runners (among the healthiest athletes) have a resting pulse rate in the 40 to 50 range. During normal activities like working or climbing stairs, these athletes typically have a pulse rate in the 60 to 70 range. Doesn't it make sense that an athlete performing a task with a pulse rate of just 70 is operating more efficiently than another individual performing the same activity with a pulse rate of 90 or more?

Typically, it takes about six weeks (if you are moderately fit) and about three months (if you are totally out of condition) for you to start to see and feel the results of your aerobic exercises. This is the reason I asked you to make a commitment to exercise for three months.

It is important for you to remember that there are many components to fitness, and that no one activity will give you everything you need. Complete physical fitness includes cardiovascular endurance, muscular endurance, strength, and flexibility. It will take time and work in a variety of different disciplines before you will be able to reach your full potential. For now, however, we will focus on your cardiovascular endurance—and the way to do that is to concentrate on aerobic exercise. In later chapters I'll teach you specific ways to improve your muscular endurance, strength, and flexibility.

## Calculate your training heart rate

Simply starting a jogging program without a plan and without a goal is counterproductive. To establish a goal, you must first determine what is known as your "training" heart rate, or THR. This number is the pulse rate that allows you to achieve maximum cardiovascular benefits without running the risk of injury or overexertion.

Begin by finding out what your maximum achieved heart rate is with a stress test. Once you know what your maximum achieved heart rate is, you can easily determine exactly what your THR should be: 60 percent of your maximum heart rate during your first month of exercise; 70 percent during your second month; and 80 percent during your third month.

If you have not had a stress test, there are several formulas you can use to calculate your THR. The simplest formula—for healthy individuals—is to base it on your age. Here's how it works:

You subtract your age from 220 and multiply that number by:
- 60 percent during your first month of exercise,
- 70 percent during your second month of exercise, and
- 80 percent during your third month of exercise.

For example, if you're 49 years old, you would calculate your THR by subtracting 49 (your age) from 220. That would give you a maximal heart rate of 171. Then:

- During your first month of exercise, multiply 171 by 60% = 102 (your THR for the first month).
- During your second month of exercise, multiply 171 by 70% = 120 (your THR for the second month).
- During your third month of exercise, multiply 171 by 80% = 137 (your THR for the third month).

If you have been exercising regularly, you should jump immediately to the THR calculated for your third month.

I like to think of the THR as a tool, not as a goal. So do not be concerned if you cannot maintain your exact THR when you exercise. If possible, just try to stay within 10 beats of this number. If you find that you cannot perform even minimal exercise for more than a few minutes without your pulse going way above your THR, it probably means that you are less conditioned than you thought. Another possibility is that you have a primary lung, heart, or other physiologic condition that needs to be addressed by a physician or medical specialist. In the event your pulse is way above your THR, stop the program until you get medical clearance.

## Don't push yourself

You may think your beginning THR is too low and, in fact, some individuals could start with higher rates. My experience has shown, however, that men or women who start with higher rates run the risk of injury without achieving fitness any more quickly. More important, most people who push themselves initially are the ones who quit. They do so from boredom or because they set unrealistic goals and give up rather than admit failure. So, use the THR prescribed for your age, using the formula above, and you'll find that exercise can be both beneficial and painless.

Remember that word "painless." It's important.

In fact, one thing that most of my cardiac patients notice, once they've been exercising for just a few weeks, is that they have not experienced the soreness that they expected when they started to exercise. They appreciate being able to achieve fitness without going through days when they're so sore they can't walk. (I wish I could teach this lesson to directors of health clubs who believe that pain is a necessary ingredient of physical conditioning.)

In my opinion, people experience muscle soreness only when they try to achieve goals they're not ready to achieve. It is for this reason that I like to keep the THR on the low side and focus on this training rate rather than on an ultimate target.

Today, for example, I had a great workout. It was a sunny day and I decided to go for a four-mile walk/jog instead of my usual cycling workout. During most of that time, I got my pulse rate up to only 118–122. Yet I felt so invigorated at the end of the four miles.

My usual THR is between 135 and 150 when I'm riding or running hard. But workouts like this one, when I don't push myself to the limit, are my most memorable. Learn to enjoy your training and you will heighten your personal sense of well-being even if you don't reach your THR.

## Taking the Pulse of Your Workout

The best way to monitor your training heart rate is to get a pulse watch. (I use one made by Polar.) With this simple device, you wear a band around your chest and a battery-operated sensor in the band sends your pulse to a watch you wear on your wrist. In this way, you can safely exercise while monitoring your pulse rate at or near your THR.

If you do not have a pulse watch, there are two places on your body where you can conveniently and easily take your own pulse: the radial artery at the wrist and the carotid artery at the neck.

To take your pulse at the wrist: It is simpler and safer to measure your pulse here. Place one hand in a relaxed, palm-up position. Then gently press the softest parts of the index and middle fingers of your other hand onto the base of the thumb (where your wrist bone joins your wrist). Do not press too hard, and don't try to get a reading with your thumb. You'll feel the pulse like a gentle drumbeat. Using a watch, count the number of beats you feel for 10 seconds. Multiply that number by six to get your pulse rate.

To take your carotid artery pulse: Place the same two fingers about one inch below the angle of the jaw bone in front of the sternocleidomastoid muscle, which is the large muscle in the front of your neck (or just in front of that point). When taking your pulse this way, it is extremely important not to press too hard or to make any sudden motions with your neck, or you might reduce the blood flow to your brain and become dizzy. Count the number of beats in 10 seconds and then multiply by six.

If you can't find your radial or carotid pulse, ask a nurse, physician, or friend who has been trained in first aid to help you.

## Keep a heart-rate log

I find that it's extremely valuable to keep a heart-rate log during your exercise program. The best way is to track your heart rate at rest, during training, and during recovery, keeping track of the dates and time spent exercising. You might also want to note how you felt in general: were you recovering from a cold, or coming off a hectic stretch of work? You should also record how you're exercising—whether you were running or cycling, for example. Use your log for your first three to six months of exercise and you'll learn a great deal about yourself and the way your body is changing.

To fill in your log, take your pulse each morning before getting out of bed and record it as your resting pulse rate. Take your pulse at the beginning of each exercise session, at each session's mid-point, and within five minutes following each session. This last measurement is your recovery heart rate.

## What the numbers mean

Your resting heart rate gives you an idea of your current physical condition. It also gives you a way to track your progress. Your heart rate will almost certainly be higher than the 40 to 60 beats per minute of a world-class athlete the first time you take it, but as you exercise aerobically, you'll see that number steadily decline. In addition, your resting heart rate gives you a way to assess your stress level and to recognize overtraining.

Your training heart rate is your guide while you are exercising. If your heart rate is far above your THR, slow down. If your heart rate is within 10 beats of your THR, you are exercising safely, without putting undue strain on your heart. Your THR is a tool you can use to avoid unwanted anaerobic activity and to avoid muscle soreness.

Here's one way to tell without checking your pulse whether you've gone above your THR: You should be able to exercise with so little strain that you could carry on a conversation without gasping for breath.

Your recovery heart rate, taken within five minutes of the end of your session, also lets you know if you are overexerting yourself. This rate should fall to 100 or below within five minutes. If it doesn't, either you've exercised

## How I Use My Heart-Rate Log

My resting heart rate in the morning is between 48 and 55. If I wake up and my pulse is 60, I know that something has overtaxed my system. So if I'm scheduled for a strenuous exercise routine, I don't do it. I know that by exerting myself when my heart rate is higher than normal, I am risking injury and/or illness. My resting heart rate warns me that something is going on, even if I'm not yet aware of what it might be.

After my workout, my pulse rate normally falls to 98 or so within two minutes. If it takes six or seven minutes for me to recover, I know that something is wrong. Since I live in Florida, one possibility is that the temperature and humidity are higher than I anticipated, and I'm dehydrated. That means I need to drink more water during my run or start hydrating beforehand to prevent the risk of dehydration. Another possibility is that my recovery is not normal because I've pushed myself too far.

too vigorously, or there is some other reason your pulse is too high. Take it easy. If your rate still doesn't drop after you moderate your exercise intensity, see your physician and explain what's happening.

I strongly recommend that you use such a log. It will help you to become aware of how much more efficient your body can be after just three months of aerobics. If, for example, you start with a resting heart rate of 90 and see it steadily decline over a period of three months until it's down to 75 or 80, you'll have proof in writing of one of the results of your exercise regimen. You'll know how much work you're saving your heart each and every day. And you'll be much more likely to continue exercising for the rest of your long, healthy life.

Your log will also show you how quickly you can lose valuable ground. If you exercise for just a few weeks and then stop for a period of time, it will be reflected in your heart rate log.

## The power of perseverance

Of course, no amount of preparation or calculation will do any good unless you continue to exercise once you begin.

In the beginning, schedule your exercise sessions like regular appointments. Write them down in your calendar. Call your own answering machine to confirm them. If you miss a day, make it up that same week. Stick to your schedule until exercise becomes a habit.

The most common reason people quit exercising is boredom. That's why it's so important for you to find an activity you truly enjoy and will continue to enjoy over the long haul. Find the right exercise—walking, running or jogging, cycling, aerobic dance, cross-country skiing, or swimming—and then stick with it. If you enjoy more than one activity, alternate them weekly or from session to session. If you hate to exercise alone, find a partner—your spouse, a friend, your child, or even your dog. Many of my patients have enrolled in classes where they were able to mix socializing and exercising.

Try a variety of classes, including step aerobics, exercycle "spinning," water aerobics, kickboxing, or Tae-Bo. Tai chi and yoga can be considered aerobic when done properly. And my trainer, Carl Bousquet has convinced me that it is even possible to get aerobic conditioning from weight training, as long as you move continuously, taking short rests and doing high numbers of repetitions, or use a circuit weight training class.

Do whatever you have to do to make yourself exercise. Even if you're not having fun, do it anyway. Get started doing something while you figure out what will make it fun. It's the single most important physical commitment you can make on your journey to a healthy life at 100.

## A way to keep improving

Your personal aerobic exercise prescription is a combination of the mode of exercise you have chosen (walking, cycling, swimming, jogging, etc.), your frequency, or number of days per week that you exercise, plus your intensity (the level of exercise necessary for you to reach your training heart rate, plus how many minutes you do per session). A typical exercise prescription might be:

Mode: exercycle

Frequency: 3 days per week

Intensity: to a THR of 129 beats per minute, or to a

speed of 15 miles per hour on the exercycle
Time: 45 minutes

In order to continue to make progress, however, you can't just keep your prescription the same. After three months on this prescription, you would increase your frequency to five days a week, or increase your intensity to

## Two Essentials: The Warm-Up and Cool-Down

**The Warm-Up:** 5 to 10 minutes. Any athlete knows that you don't just hurl your body from rest into exercise. It's necessary to warm up first. There is some controversy as to whether it is better to walk or ride a bicycle to warm your muscles before stretching, or to stretch before walking. In my opinion, if you are physically active, you know your body better than anyone else. So you be the judge. I do believe, however, that it is important to do some sort of flexibility exercise and to gently warm up on a treadmill or exercycle (or even walk) before you go out for a run. An excellent warm-up is the Sun Salutation described in Chapter 9. Then you should walk for two to five minutes before beginning your jog or ride.

**The Cool-Down:** 5 to 10 minutes. If irregular heartbeats are going to occur, they usually occur because an individual has skipped a cool-down period. If you jog or run, for example, several minutes of gradually slower walking is the ideal cool-down. If you dance or use an exercise machine, slowly jog in place for a few minutes before you completely relax or jump into a shower.

achieve a higher pulse rate, or increase your time to 60 minutes at 15 mph.

If you want to exercise more often than three times a week, I recommend that you change your mode on the extra exercise days so that you train different muscle groups. You could, for example, cycle three days and walk two, or alternate cycling with swimming.

With aerobics, total time spent exercising is more important than the distance traveled. It's more important to exercise continuously for 30 minutes than to run a quick two miles. Set a time for your jog or walk—say 40 minutes total, or 20 minutes away from your house and 20 minutes back. That way you won't have to worry about how much distance you're covering. When you are ready for more exercise, increase the time.

Harder is not always better as you progress. Many people think they're improving their routines on exercycles or rowing machines by increasing the weight, or resistance. But increasing resistance places much more strain on your heart than just increasing the frequency of arm or leg revolutions.

A better approach, for example, would be to increase your pedal revolutions from 70 to 80 per minute, or your rowing strokes from 20 to 40 per minute. Whenever you work out too hard or too often, you risk injury. And while the injury itself is painful, it may also harm you by temporarily derailing your exercise program.

The most common exercise injuries are usually caused by breaking in a new piece of equipment, such as new running shoes or a new bicycle, or by starting a new type of activity. Take it easy when you begin any new routine— and ignore the erroneous and dangerous concept of "no pain, no gain."

There are safe ways to ease into new forms of exercise. You can take courses, seek out health clubs where you can get instruction, hire a one-on-one trainer for a lesson or two, or join a cycling or running club that has a training course for beginners.

You have a lifetime to become physically conditioned—so take your time and do it safely.

## Tips for whatever exercise you choose

Here are some strategies that I recommend for specific sports.

• If you've chosen to do something that requires skill such as swimming or cross-country skiing, consider taking lessons.

• If you're chosen walking as your aerobic exercise, make sure your walks are brisk enough to help you reach your training heart rate. A brisk arm swing increases your energy needs and makes walking more vigorous. If you carry hand-held, 1- to 5-pound weights, you can increase the intensity of your walking workout even more. But you must pump the weights as you walk, however—don't just hold them.

• Jogging, while excellent aerobically, does nothing to strengthen your upper body or your quadriceps muscles (those on the front of the thigh). To strengthen the quad-criceps, try cycling, Rollerblading, or ice skating.

• If you jog more than 30 miles a week, you run the risk of knee injury. (And never jog with hand weights; this also increases your risk of knee injury.)

• Aerobic dance presents as much potential for injury as running, especially if done more then three times a week. Aerobic dance is best done with the supervision of a professional.

• Swimming is an excellent aerobic exercise, combining low injury potential and a high degree of flexibility. Plus, it

## Exercise in Safety and Comfort

Here are some tips for avoiding injuries during aerobics.

• Hydrate, hydrate, hydrate. Drink 8 to 12 ounces of water before you start exercising, and at least 8 ounces of water every 20 minutes during your workout, regardless of whether it takes place indoors or outdoors. (You don't need sports drinks or anything containing sugar unless you are exercising in excess of two hours.) Cold water is absorbed more rapidly on warm or hot days.

• If you live in a hot climate, avoid outdoor exercise when humidity is high, or you will dehydrate quickly. Instead, move your workout to an air-conditioned mall, YMCA, or your air-conditioned home.

• Choose appropriate clothing. Wear layers in cold weather so you can remove them as you warm up. In hot weather, wear clothing that is ventilated to keep your body temperature from rising. And always wear suitable exercise footwear for your workout—running shoes for running, cycling shoes for cycling, aerobic shoes for aerobics, and cross-training shoes for both running and cycling.

• Change the routine. To avoid injury, alternate days of hard exercise with days of easy exercise. For example, if you cycle 40 miles one day, make the next day a rest day or a day on which you go for a 20- or 25-mile ride.

• Go with the flow. If there is a wind blowing, start your exercise into the wind so that your return trip will be more comfortable.

exercises both your upper and lower body muscles. But take lessons to learn to do the strokes correctly. Alternate between a work stroke (such as freestyle) and a rest stroke (such as side stroke) so you will be able to swim for 30 consecutive minutes or more.

• Bicycling is another great aerobic sport. To improve conditioning while avoiding injury, use spinning—a technique of pedaling an exercycle between 70 and 100 revolutions per minute. Toe clips or specialized pedals can improve your exercise efficiency by making sure both the quadriceps and hamstring muscles are worked. During all cycling, keep your knees in close and your heels flat.

• Cross-country skiing exercises both your arms and legs vigorously. The popular machines that simulate the motions of cross-country skiing provide a less strenuous exercise. But it may be too strenuous for those individuals with heart or lung problems.

• Kickboxing and Tae-Bo have become very popular in the past two years. But in my experience, they are associated with a high injury risk in people who are not already physically fit. My recommendation is to wait until you have been exercising for at least three to six months before trying one of these classes.

• Keep in mind that some of the Eastern forms of exercise can be extremely beneficial in maintaining aerobic conditioning. Yoga and tai chi are considered to be complete exercises because they increase flexibility, increase strength, and increase cardiovascular endurance. Ask your instructor about using these forms for aerobic exercise.

## My bargain with you

Here's a deal for you: If you start your program, stick with it for three months, and do not notice a significant change in the way you feel and/or look, you can stop exercising.

If, on the other hand, you do notice a significant change—if you've got more energy, if you look younger and more vital—then you have to renew your contract for another full year!

Naturally, my ultimate goal is to convince you to exercise for the rest of your life. Right now, however, I'm not asking you for that kind of long-term commitment. Instead, I'm asking you to put into action the contract you signed back in Chapter 3: to exercise aerobically according to my "Rule of 3s."

I want you to choose an aerobic exercise now and to participate in that exercise for 30 to 60 minutes, three times a week, for three months.

This is the least you can do to achieve positive results. If you are completely out of shape, it may take you as long as three weeks before you can comfortably exercise for a full 30 minutes. Once you reach that stage, though, 30 minutes is your minimum.

## A slow but sure victory

I know a 57-year-old physician who, in 1970, at the age of 45, began a simple aerobic program of jogging for 30 minutes three times a week. In 1975, when he had a stress test, he lasted 12 minutes on the treadmill. When he repeated the treadmill test in 1979, he lasted 15 minutes. In 1982, he went 19 minutes and 18 seconds. This represents an increase in his maximal oxygen utilization from approximately 35 milliliters of oxygen per kilogram of body weight in 1975, to 61 milliliters of oxygen per kilogram of body weight in 1982. In other words, in 12 years he nearly doubled how much oxygen his heart can deliver to his body!

It may be hard to believe that slow, regular activity can make a 57-year-old male more fit than most men in their 20s, but that is exactly what it did in this case. This man's experience also confirms that it is not necessary to exercise every day, and that it is not necessary to spend hours and hours running, cycling, or swimming.

If you perform your aerobic exercise regularly—following my "Rule of 3s," you will have the same positive results.

## What else you'll see change

Here's what you can expect if you make aerobic exercise a part of your life:
• A stronger, more efficient heart. At rest, your heart rate will be about 10 to 20 beats-per-minute lower than the heart rate of an unconditioned man or woman. When you exercise, even full tilt, your heart won't pound painfully because it will be moving your blood more easily through your cardiovascular system.

• An increase in lung efficiency and capacity. Your lungs won't have to work so hard to supply your body with the oxygen you need. Even when you exercise or do physical labor, you won't get out of breath so easily. You'll be able to do more without getting tired—like you did when you were in your 20s.

• An increase in blood volume. Your body will produce more blood plasma, hemoglobin, and red blood cells (oxygen "carriers") in its drive to become ever more efficient.

• Better muscle tone and condition. Your body will look better, tighter, as you change fat weight to lean weight.

• Lower blood pressure. Your vascular system will improve as your blood vessels get stronger and increase in number in order to carry more oxygen throughout your body. As a result, your blood pressure will drop.

• Increased disease protection. As you improve your body's efficiency, strengthen your heart and lungs, and improve your muscle tone, you'll be setting up a strong line of defense against a variety of diseases—not the least of which is heart disease.

## The best reason to exercise

Adding years to your life is not the only reason to exercise. In fact, it's not even the most important reason. The most important reason is that a program of regular aerobic exercise will vastly improve the quality of your life.

Now, this is a claim that can't be quantified—it's too subjective. But I defy you to find a man or woman who exercises regularly that does not believe that exercise enhances his or her life.

I know that exercise improves the quality of life because I used to be a couch potato. And now that I exercise on a daily basis, I know I feel better, stronger, and happier as a result.

The fact is that exercise makes us feel more astute, more capable of achieving our dreams and goals. It makes us feel fully alive and in control of our own destinies. These benefits can be yours as well with aerobic exercise. It's that simple.

# CHAPTER 6

# ANTIOXIDANTS

*In the 30 years that I have been practicing medicine, I have never been more excited about the future of health care in the United States. I have always believed that living a very long life, and being healthy for all of it, was a reasonable goal. Today, there is proof that it is reasonable.*

*That proof is embodied in the discovery of one of the main molecular enemies of health: the free radical. Because now that we know how this health thief works, we also know that we have a fantastically effective weapon against it.*

Free radicals—the unique health-stealing molecules that I'm going to tell you about in this chapter—have been linked (at last count) to about 80 diseases. Antioxidants can prevent, stop, and in some cases even reverse the damage done by free radicals.

This discovery is as important to the health and well-being of men and women all around the world as was the discovery of penicillin or the discovery that simple sterilization techniques would stop infection in operating rooms. It makes it crystal clear that if you want to live long enough to dance the polka at your great-great-grandson's wedding, you'd better start an immediate regimen to make sure you get all the antioxidants you need.

## Just what are free radicals?

Try to imagine a Viking horde at work inside your body. Imagine this army attacking and damaging healthy cells, breaking down the collagen that keeps your skin firm and youthful, attacking your eyes so that you develop cataracts, working away inside your circulatory system to cause heart disease and stroke, joining forces with cigarette smoke to increase your risk of lung cancer (if you're a smoker), and so on.

That's a simple way to visualize free radicals.

In more scientific terms, free radicals are highly unstable oxygen molecules. Normal metabolism—just your body going about its day-to-day work of storing and burning energy—creates these free radicals as a byproduct.

Unlike stable molecules, which have electrons that are paired so that their positive and negative electrical charges cancel each other out, a free radical has an unpaired, electrically charged electron that is hungry for a mate. Free radicals do their damage by stealing electrons from stable molecules.

This theft turns these molecules into new free radicals that, in turn, must prey on other stable molecules—and so on. As a result, normal body structures break down and don't repair themselves. This free-radical chain reaction can puncture cell membranes, allowing fluids to leak out and disrupting the ability of the cell to take in nutrients. It can even break up the body's DNA and RNA—the basic building blocks of genetics—creating mutations that reproduce uncontrollably.

If you want to see free radicals at work, cut an apple in half. After a few minutes, you'll see the apple start to turn brown. What you're watching here is the process of free radicals from oxygen in the air attacking and changing the molecular structure of the fruit by "stealing" electrons from healthy molecules.

However, if you put the juice of a lemon, which is loaded with vitamin C, on the cut surfaces of the apple, you will neutralize the process, or at least you'll slow it down. That's how antioxidants like vitamin C work.

Brown, discolored fruit is, at worst, distasteful. But what free radicals do in your body is downright deadly.

## So what's a body to do?

Well, you can't live without oxygen. It's the fuel for your cells, and your body can't function without it. At the same time, that life-sustaining oxygen in your system is creating cell-destroying free radicals.

However, every organism that depends on oxygen for fuel has a built-in system to diffuse the damage done by that oxygen. The more efficient the system, the longer they live. Mice, for example, sustain ten times the number of injuries on the DNA molecule that humans do, and thus have a relatively short lifespan.

Compared to most other animals, humans are relatively good at protecting against free-radical damage. We have three lines of defense.

First, we have a system of enzymes, molecular machinery built by the body to specifications to maintain DNA. These enzymes take free radicals apart and render them harmless.

Within this enzymatic line of defense, there are three

## Two Antioxidant Pioneers: Drs. Harman and Pauling

If, like most people, you've gotten whatever information you have about free radicals and antioxidants from the popular press and television, you probably think free radicals were just discovered a few years ago. In fact, the theory that free radicals are linked to aging and death was first put forward more than 40 years ago by Dr. Denham Harman of the University of Nebraska.

At that time, Dr. Harman's theory was viewed by some to be the product of a crackpot mind. In Dr. Harman's words, when he told his theory to colleagues in Berkeley, California, in December of 1954, "the general reaction was negative." At best, it was considered to be little more than another interesting hypothesis in the study of aging, a field that has long been filled with hypotheses.

It was Dr. Harman's theory that free-radical reactions may play a role in at least 80 diseases, including cancer, heart attacks, stroke, rheumatoid arthritis, cataracts, and Alzheimer's disease—the major cause of admissions to nursing homes today.

But Harman's work remained an interesting hypothesis was largely what this remained until the 1980s or so, when an increasing number of scientists started their own experiments into the causes and prevention of aging. Those experiments, in turn, have produced growing enthusiasm for the propositions first put forward by Dr. Harman in the 1950s.

Another expert in the field of antioxidants, Linus Pauling, Ph.D., is probably best known for his research on the antioxidant vitamin C, although he received the Nobel Peace Prize in 1962 for his work to ban nuclear bomb testing. Here's what Dr. Pauling said in an interview about the relationship between vitamin C and heart disease:

> ...it was accepted by cardiologists that the primary cause of atherosclerosis and heart disease is a lesion in the wall of an artery in a region of stress. So I asked myself . . . , "why should there be a lesion in the wall of the artery?" Animals don't have these lesions in regions of stress. Well, you have the lesions because arteries are weak.
>
> Why are they weak? Ordinarily, animals' arteries are strengthened by the deposit of collagen. And you can't make collagen without using up vitamin C. Humans don't get enough vitamin C, so their arteries are weak. And then a lesion forms, followed by the other stages of developing heart disease. Therefore, deficient intake of vitamin C is a primary cause of cardiovascular disease.

Before his death, Dr. Pauling made the statement that 10 to 20 grams of vitamin C per day would control cardiovascular disease and would improve the results of cancer therapy. Yet, like Dr. Pauling, I find that the medical establishment, despite all of the research, is still holding on to the idea that food is the only source of vitamins, and that antioxidants taken in supplement form are of little or no benefit. I believe that since we don't produce vitamin C in the liver, it is necessary for us to get this vitamin from another source.

Both Harman and Pauling took vitamins themselves. While there are many rumors about Pauling's intake, it is now believed he took around 20 grams, or 20,000 milligrams, a day. Physicians now recommend no more than 500 miligrams a day. As for Harman, when he was asked by interviewer Dr. Richard Passwater what his personal vitamin regimen was, he said that he took 200 milligrams of vitamin E per day, 10 milligrams of CoQ10 with each meal, one yeast tablet (for chromium) containing 50 micrograms of selenium twice a day, and one multivitamin tablet.

major enzymes. Superoxide dismutase (SOD) focuses on defusing the master free radical, superoxide. Catalase specializes in rendering hydrogen peroxide harmless. Finally, glutathione peroxidase tackles both hydrogen peroxide and the lipid peroxides that are generated in cell membranes.

Our second line of defense consists of a wide range of internally created biomolecules that sacrifice an electron to neutralize the hungry free radicals and become free radicals themselves. In this process, less crucial cells are sacrificed while crucial cells are protected. This system does not work as well as the enzyme system. It neutralizes the free radicals, but it changes the optimum functioning of the body's cells in the process.

Our last line of defense is provided by nutrients. These supplemental reinforcements also work through the sacrificial mode. For example, vitamin E can attach itself to a free radical and neutralize the free radical so that it can't do any damage. However, sometimes in this process, the vitamin E molecule itself becomes a free radical. When this happens, the molecule that results is called a reactive oxygen species (ROS). These molecules also have free electrons and can cause damage.

The first of these defense systems is the most effective. Molecule for molecule, the body's own enymes work better than sacrificial biochemicals or nutrients. However, our levels of these enzymes decline as we age. For now, the use of nutrients, from both foods and supplements, is the best way I know of to help our bodies intervene and disrupt the process of destruction by free radicals.

## Free radicals, antioxidants, and disease

Our first evidence of the value of an ingestible antioxidant is with selenium, an important component of glutathione. It appears that people who live in areas where the soil has been depleted of selenium may actually be more susceptible to disease. In South Dakota, for example, where the selenium level of the soil is among the highest in the nation, cancer levels are among the lowest. And in Ohio, where soil is largely selenium-depleted, there is a much higher incidence of cancer.

Individuals with high levels of selenium in their blood have low cancer rates, and doctors consider a low level of selenium in the blood indicates cancer risk. Ingesting selenium also protects the liver from carbon tetrachloride. And it plays a protective role against the hepatitis B virus and primary liver cancer.

Researchers now have proven that free radicals can attack low-density lipoprotein (LDL), the "bad" cholesterol, and change it into a form that damages the lining of the coronary arteries. The body, in response, patches the damaged arterial lining with a fatty deposit that narrows the arteries and ultimately leads to heart disease.

Just as a build-up of plaque in the coronary arteries leads to heart attack, so a build-up of this gunk in cerebral arteries can lead to what doctors euphemistically call a "cerebral accident" or stroke. Scientists haven't yet officially connected this type of build-up to free radicals, but it makes sense to me—common sense—that if free radicals can cause plaque in coronary arteries, they'll cause the same kind of plaque formation in other arteries.

All strokes are not due to a build-up of plaque in the arteries in or to the brain. But there's no doubt that free radicals do damage to the vessel walls—and a damaged arterial wall can bleed into the brain, causing a stroke.

Scientists also know that free radicals have the ability to

change a cell's DNA in a way that can make healthy cells become cancerous. They know that continued free radical damage has been linked to breast, lung, and colon cancers—three diseases that account for about half of all cancer deaths in the U.S. each year.

Finally, scientists believe that free radical damage is responsible for many other diseases and conditions long thought to be a normal part of the aging process. They include cataracts, wrinkling and skin discoloration, even senility, diabetes, inflammatory bowel disease, pancreatic inflammation, and peptic ulcers also may be linked to free radical damage.

## You shouldn't be willing to wait

Scientists will give us the official word on the cause-and-effect relationship between free radicals and disease in 10 years or so. But I'm not willing to wait that long. And you shouldn't be willing to wait either, because there are things you can do—today—to combat any possible damage being done by free radicals in your body. You can take action today that will—I believe with all my heart—not only give you protection from a wide variety of illnesses and debilitating conditions associated with aging, but also will ward off and even reverse the damage done by these voracious agents of age and decay.

Theories abound concerning just how and why antioxidants fight aging and disease. Some of the most intriguing ongoing research—being conducted by the National Institute on Aging—indicates that when a cell line (the multi-generational "family" of cells that's formed as cells divide and re-divide over time) is young, the enzymes we know as antioxidants naturally disarm and make harmless free radicals.

Over time, though, these enzymes appear to lose their ability to counteract the effects of free radicals.

One of the most graphic studies for illustrating what antioxidants can do for you was undertaken by Dr. Rajindar Sohal and Dr. William Orr, biologists at Southern Methodist University. They published their results in the journal *Science* in late February 1994.

In the Sohal-Orr study, fruit flies were given extra copies of genes that produced two enzymes: SOD to convert free radicals to hydrogen peroxide, and catalase to convert hydrogen peroxide to water. The result was truly remarkable. The flies that were given the extra genes lived 30 percent longer than those that did not receive the genes. In addition, according to the researchers, the genetically altered fruit flies were more spry, vigorous, and nimble while they were alive. In other words, they stayed younger.

In fact, said Sohal, "We could tell which ones [were given the free radical-fighting genes] just by looking at them."

To be sure, this experiment was on fruit flies, not humans. However, humans and flies have almost identical systems for dealing with and defusing free radicals. But don't let this one study convince you. Take a look at some of the other research that's been done on antioxidants, free radicals, and disease.

## Heart disease and heart attack

A joint study by the Harvard School of Public Health and Boston's Brigham and Women's Hospital tracked the course of more than 87,000 women and 45,000 men who had no history of heart disease to see if taking the antioxidant vitamin E would have any effect on their risk of developing the disease. The bottom line? Women who took more than 100 I.U. of vitamin E for more than two years had about half the risk of heart disease as women who didn't. Men who took the same dose over the same period reduced their risk by more than 25 percent.

Researchers at Loma Linda University studied the connection between diet and death in 27,529 California Seventh Day Adventist adults over a period of two decades. The Adventists made nearly perfect research subjects, because they follow strict dietary practices that set them apart from the general U.S. population. They don't eat pork or drink alcohol, for example, and are urged not to eat meat, fish, or eggs. They also avoid smoking, coffee, and spices.

That survey showed, beyond any doubt, that a vegetarian diet—which just happens to be loaded with antioxidants that protect against free radicals—resulted in lower death rates from coronary disease in both men and women.

## Stroke

The Harvard Medical School/Boston Hospital study mentioned above also showed that women who ate five or more servings per week of carrots (one of the vegetables high in the antioxidants vitamin C and beta-carotene) had a 68 percent lower risk of stroke than women who ate no more than one serving per month.

Another study, conducted at the University of Tennessee in Memphis, showed that men and women who had the highest intake of vitamin E had the least thickening of the walls of the arteries leading to the brain, and, thus, a significantly lower risk of stroke.

## Senility

A National Academy of Science study showed that administering the antioxidant agent PBN to elderly gerbils decreased the amount of free radical-damaged tissue in the animals' brains and actually reversed memory loss (as measured by a maze test). In fact, after two weeks of treatment with PBN, the old gerbils in the test had mental acuity similar to that of young animals. Once the PBN was discontinued, the animals rapidly started aging once again.

This is an example of the kind of study that many in the medical community would say has little, if any, relevance to us. After all, gerbils aren't humans. But I believe that the results of this study lead straight to the commonsense conclusion that if I boost my antioxidant intake, through diet and dietary supplements, I will be able to ward off the effects of aging.

## Cancer

A study conducted by the National Cancer Institute found that people who regularly took 100 I.U. of vitamin E along with other supplements had about half the risk of developing cancer of the mouth and throat than those who did not take the vitamin E supplements.

Another study, this one jointly sponsored by the NCI and several Chinese medical research institutions, tracked 30,000 Chinese men and women. It gave them daily doses of vitamin E and the mineral selenium along with beta-carotene over a five-year period. The group getting the antioxidants showed a decrease of 13 percent in their overall cancer risk compared with a group that was given placebos. Of even more interest to researchers, those who received beta-carotene had a 21 percent reduction in risk of stomach cancer, the most common form of cancer in China.

These results, researchers noted, might have been slightly skewed because being in the study itself improved the general nutritional levels of participants. However, the results offer real hope that vitamins and minerals may be effective in reducing cancer.

Still another study on cancer showed that daily doses of beta carotene actually had the ability to heal mouth lesions in some cigarette smokers—and that those lesions would reappear once the beta-carotene intake stopped.

Meanwhile, the Loma Linda study on Seventh-Day Adventists also pointed out the value of a vegetarian diet in battling cancer. Both male and female vegetarians in that study had lower death rates for colon cancer, and the women had lower death rates for ovarian cancer.

It is these studies and many others like them, showing the ability of vitamins, nutrients, and herbs to counteract the damaging effects of free radicals, that have led me to trumpet the discovery of antioxidants as the most important health discovery of the past 50 years.

## Should you wait for more research?

I'll admit, up front and at the outset, that the information we have about free radicals isn't exact or complete. Research scientists around the world and practitioners like me are uncovering and discovering new facts each and every day. What I'm putting in your hands is the very latest information that's available today.

However, it's important for you to realize that the minute this book goes into print, new information will become available. To provide my readers, on an ongoing basis, with the latest findings on the prevention and treatment of disease with alternative mind-body medicine, I began to write my newsletter, "Health & Longevity," in 1993. This is one of a handful of publications that bring you the most up-to-date scientific research in way that you can use it.

Your only other choice is to wait the 10 years or more it will take for the medical community to jump on the free radical/antioxidant bandwagon. You can wait for a final okay from the American Medical Association before you take action to stop the damage being done to your body every day by free radicals. However, it is my belief that if you delay and don't take the few simple actions I'll tell you about to stop free radicals cold—and even reverse the damage they've already done to your body—you'll be turning your back on the greatest preventive-therapeutic tool in the history of medicine.

## What you can do about free radicals

It's not just your own metabolic processes that produce free radicals in your body. The pesticides in our food, the hole in the ozone, a diet high in saturated fats, too little exercise, too much exercise, excessive body fat, too much radiation, drugs that we take for high blood pressure and other maladies, chemotherapeutic agents used for cancer, margarine and butter, too much sunlight—these are all additional free-radical injuries that our bodies have to endure. All of these factors lead to what practitioners call "oxidative stress"—the wear and tear of living.

As you begin your journey to a healthy life at 100, understand that you're going to have to pay attention to

## Why You Didn't Hear About Antioxidants Sooner

Until very recently, much of the experimental laboratory work undertaken to find out exactly how and why free radicals scavenge the body, and—more important—how we can ward off their attacks, has been largely unreported in the non-scientific press. But, you might ask, why isn't this news being shouted from the rooftops? Why are most people only now beginning to learn about free radicals and antioxidants?

The medical community is ultra-conservative when it comes to making new ideas and new therapies available to the public. Scientists want to be 100-percent certain of their findings before they release them. Wrong conclusions can have tragic consequences. On the other hand, scientists can have a "blind spot" when it comes to any discoveries that challenge long-accepted beliefs.

This ultra-conservatism, while often justified, can be carried to extremes. And that, in my estimation, is exactly what's happening with research into free radicals and antioxidants. The medical community—not entirely, but in the main—is being overly conservative by not trumpeting the news that you can, indeed, expect to live to be 120 if you take some relatively simple steps.

The medical establishment is dragging its feet even in the face of what I view as overwhelming evidence linking free radicals to aging and death and linking antioxidants to longer, healthier life spans. Unfortunately, most of the evidence uncovered so far has not been the result of traditional research methods. Instead, it is what we might call "commonsense evidence."

For example, a study of a large group of nurses at the Harvard School of Public Health showed that taking 100 I.U. of vitamin E daily reduced the risk of heart disease in those nurses by almost 50 percent. Common sense, then, would indicate that taking the antioxidant vitamin E would, at the very least, help lower the risk of heart attack. This evidence, though, was not the product of what one researcher called the "gold standard" of medical research—a controlled clinical trial with two large groups of individuals randomly selected either to receive vitamin E, or to receive no supplement, or to receive a placebo. As a result, the Harvard Study is largely discounted by most in the medical community.

More recently, a 1999 article proposed that multiple antioxidant vitamin supplements together with diet and lifestyle modifications may improve the efficacy of both standard and experimental cancer therapies. Despite the evidence presented in this article—evidence showing that antioxidant vitamins improve cell function and reduce the toxicity of chemotherapeutic agents—oncologists still tell their patients to avoid antioxidants while they are undergoing chemotherapy.

Since the "gold standard" of research was not used in these studies—and many others like them—the medical community, as a whole, won't come out and openly endorse the idea that free radicals are the agents of aging, disease, and death until the evidence of randomized clinical studies is so staggering that it can no longer be questioned on any level. And that's likely to take at least another decade.

In the meantime, of course, people are growing older and weaker. They're suffering from disease and illness—and they're dying from a lack of available information.

But you don't have to be one of those people.

your lifestyle and avoid excessive free-radical injuries. This means putting a hat on in the sun, avoiding exposure to toxic chemicals, and quitting smoking. It also means paying attention to the food you put into your body. Some foods actually cause free-radical injury and some foods provide you with extra antioxidants.

But lifestyle habits can be slow to change. That's why I'm going to talk to you first about boosting your antioxidant intake with supplements. It doesn't mean you're off the hook for improving your lifestyle; I'm just being realistic about what changes you can make for yourself *today*.

## My top 10 antioxidant supplements

These are the antioxidant supplements that I believe should be taken on a regular basis to help protect against free-radical damage. I'll talk to you about each of them in detail, giving you my suggested dosage for each of them. Some of these antioxidants can be found in food sources, and I'll briefly mention what those sources are. Then I'll talk to you about antioxidants in your diet at the end of this chapter.

### Coenzyme Q10

This compound is found in every living plant and animal cell. In a sense, it's a part of the mitochondria, the energy-producing unit of the cells of the body. Dr. Denham Harman said that CoQ10 is more than an antioxidant: it is the only substance that slows down mitochondrial degradation and therefore decreases aging. We don't know why, but the body's concentration of CoQ10 decreases with age.

CoQ10 mainly works on fat metabolism, sparing vitamin E from being used for this job. It also works with vitamin E to prevent damage to fat cell membranes. While CoQ10 is primarily helpful in the treatment of cardiovascular diseases such as angina, it also may benefit people with high blood pressure, congestive heart failure, diabetes, periodontal disease, and even cancer.

Food sources of CoQ10 are very limited: spinach, sardines, peanuts, and beef heart. Supplements are predominantly found in capsule form. This antioxidant seems to be better absorbed if formulated in a soybean oil or rice bran oil extract.

**How much you should take:** As a preventive, I believe that a milligram of CoQ10 per pound of lean body mass (body weight without body fat) is appropriate. In other words, the average individual should be taking 110 to 180 milligrams of CoQ10 per day. Therapeutically, I use CoQ10 in all patients with heart disease. Since CoQ10 has no side effects, this is one situation where a higher dose is indicated in most illnesses. For people with congestive heart failure or cardiomyopathy, I generally use two milligrams per pound of lean body mass; for those with high blood pressure, one to two milligrams per pound. For those with gum disease, I use 400 milligrams per day for six months to see if it has shown benefits by the next dental exam. In cancer therapy, I would recommend doses in excess of 600 to 800 milligrams per day.

The one situation for which most of my colleagues do not use CoQ10 is in the treatment of irregular heartbeats, especially irregular atrial beats. However, I use high doses of CoQ10 for that condition, too—roughly 300 to 400 milligrams per day in divided doses.

*Caution:* The only caution I have is that in my experience, if the CoQ10 is combined with hawthorn berry extract, it can make some conditions worse. So I don't combine them.

I use CoQ10 first, then the hawthorn extract.

## Vitamin C

Vitamin C was once known only for the prevention of scurvy. We now know that it's also beneficial in the prevention and treatment of heart disease, cancer, the common cold, cataracts, arteriosclerosis (when there's elevated cholesterol and high blood pressure), and asthma. It protects the skin against free-radical damage, and it raises levels of HDL cholesterol (the good cholesterol).

One of the interesting things about vitamin C is that it helps protect the glutathione levels of the cells. You can take 3,000 milligrams of glutathione, but your glutathione blood levels will not rise. Yet a single 500-milligram dose of vitamin C will protect your body's degradation of glutathione and increase circulating glutathione to a clinically beneficial level (as much as three grams).

This vitamin works in conjunction with vitamin E and the carotenoids to protect against free-radical damage. However, unlike these fat-soluble antioxidants, vitamin C is water soluble. That means you can safely take it in extremely high doses, because what your body doesn't use is eliminated in your urine.

**How much you should take:** For health maintenance, I use vitamin C in doses from 2,000 to 4,000 milligrams a day. For patients with a common cold, I increase that to 8,000 to 15,000 milligrams a day. For those with cancer, my protocol is to use the highest obtainable vitamin C dose to tolerance—up to 20 grams of oral vitamin C a day. ("Tolerance" is determined by the point at which the patient gets diarrhea.)

On a weekly basis, for the first six months, I treat my cancer patients with intravenous vitamin C in doses of 20 to 50 grams (20,000 to 50,000 milligrams). After six months, I reduce that to twice a month, and after one year, I reduce it further to monthly injections.

It's hard for me to understand why oncologists don't see the benefit of antioxidants in cancer therapy. I believe that every cancer patient undergoing chemotherapy, when they're on the off week, should receive an intravenous dose of vitamin C in the range of 20 to 50 grams. They should also be given ten grams of vitamin C a day to enhance the benefit of the chemotherapy (if they choose to use that therapy at all).

Dr. Linus Pauling collaborated with Dr. Ewan Cameron on the use of large doses of vitamin C in incurable cancer patients. A study on 1,500 patients found that the survival time of those who were given ten grams of vitamin C daily was almost double that of the controls (343 days vs. 180 days).

## Selenium

This trace mineral functions primarily as a component of the antioxidant enzyme system, mainly with glutathione peroxidase. It works with vitamin E in preventing free-radical damage to the cell membrane. If you have low levels of selenium, you also have a higher risk of cardiovascular disease, inflammatory disease, and cancer. Cataracts and premature aging are also linked a selenium deficiency.

Selenium is important in the treatment of AIDS, cardiovascular disease, and all inflammatory diseases. It is especially important in cancer prevention and treatment because its vital role as a component of glutathione peroxidase helps strengthen the immune system. Selenium is also important for people who've been exposed to toxic metals such as lead, mercury, aluminum, and cadmium.

**How much you should take:** My typical recommendation for health maintenance is 100 to 200 micrograms of selenium per day. In patients with HIV, I might use doses in excess of 400 to 1,000 micrograms per day.

*Caution:* In prolonged use of high-dose selenium, nervousness, irritability, nausea, vomiting, and a garlic odor of the breath and sweat may occur. However, this is very rare, and certainly nothing to worry about so long as you don't develop symptoms. If you do, consult your doctor. You'll likely want to decrease your dosage.

### Vitamin E

This vitamin partners with both vitamin C and selenium to protect cell membranes. Even in fairly low doses, it protects against heart disease and strokes because it prevents the oxidation of cholesterol and damage to the arteries. It also protects against, cancer, cataracts, diabetes, and fibrocystic breast disease. Vitamin E can even benefit people with neuromuscular diseases—fibromyalgia, multiple sclerosis, and perhaps myaestenia gravis—as well as collagen-related vascular diseases, gum diseases, and possibly even Parkinson's disease.

However, this is one of the few vitamins that must come from natural sources. The water-soluble natural form has the highest levels of active d-alpha tocopherols, so when you purchase vitamin E, this is the type to look for.

**How much you should take:** To maintain health, I recommend 400 to 500 I.U. daily. For the treatment of cancer and heart disease, take 800 to 1,200 I.U. Diabetics should take as much as 1,200 to 1,500 I.U. for two to three months at a time. I find vitamin E to be extremely helpful in the treatment of menopausal symptoms; I often prescribe 800 to 1,200 I.U. per day. I also use it for acne in children and for patients with general skin problems.

*Caution:* I believe that vitamin E is extremely safe. Though you may have heard that high doses of vitamin E can cause high blood pressure, it has been my experience that this does not occur in doses up to 1,200 I.U. per day. There have been no reports of toxicity with vitamin E; some doctors feel that doses as high as 3,000 I.U. can be tolerated. If a patient shows elevated blood pressure, however, I usually reduce the dose for a while to see if their blood pressure will return to normal.

## Vitamin A

This fat-soluble vitamin is very important in the protection of the eyes. In fact, deficiency of it can even cause blindness. Vitamin A is also important for healthy skin.

**How much you should take:** I recommend 5,000 to 10,000 I.U. of vitamin A from cod liver oil daily (that's one to three tablespoons). This form gives you the isolated pure form of vitamin A (retinol), along with plenty of omega-3 and omega-6 essential fatty acids (EFAs).

*Caution:* There have been some reports that high levels of vitamin A may cause liver damage. Even though it is rarely necessary to take more than 5,000 to 10,000 I.U. of this antioxidant, because the liver stores more than 90 percent of the vitamin A we ingest, many people worry about taking it in supplement form. In my opinion, you would have to have an extremely high level of vitamin A in your diet to sustain harm from supplements. For example, you'd have to consume four to five ounces of an extremely vitamin-A-rich food such as chili peppers every day in order to get an overdose from supplementing this vitamin. In other words, I think the toxicity issue is irrelevant.

There is some evidence that high doses of vitamin A

(in excess of 10,000 I.U. daily) may cause birth defects. So if you are pregnant, no matter how little vitamin A you consume in your diet, you should use beta-carotene supplements as an alternate source of additional vitamin A.

## Beta-carotene

There is a difference between pure vitamin A (also called retinol) and pro-vitamin A (also called carotenoids). The body converts carotenoids to vitamin A as it needs to. So the beauty of the carotenoids is that you can safely take doses as high as 300,000 I.U. Because beta-carotene is the carotenoid most efficiently converted to vitamin A, it is an excellent alternative to vitamin A therapy.

Because of its potent antioxidant capability, beta-carotene is important in immune function. Like vitamin A, it and other carotenes have a great deal to do with keeping the eyes and skin healthy. High doses of beta-carotene offer significant photosensitivity protection.

**How much you should take:** I recommend 15,000 to 25,000 I.U. of beta-carotene daily. For treatment of cancer, I use 30,000 to 100,000 I.U. along with 10,000 I.U. of vitamin A. I also use beta carotene to treat immune-deficiency problems and general skin disorders.

## Antioxidant herbs from India

In his book, *Freedom From Disease*, Hari Sharma, M.D., a former professor of pathology at Ohio State University College of Medicine, reported on a multi-university project he had organized to study Indian herbs. Dr. Sharma discovered that two ancient herbal remedies, Amrit Nectar (MAK-4) and Ambrosia (MAK-5) greatly increase the responsiveness of the immune system.

The ingredients in MAK-4 and MAK-5 are too

numerous to list, but include such things as Indian gooseberry, Indian gallnut, cardamom, cinnamon, long pepper, Indian pennywort, nutgrass, white sandalwood, and aloeweed. The herbs are delivered in a paste of clarified butter, whole cane sugar, and honey. (Though the formula is also available in capsule form, I don't think it is as effective as the original paste. I have, however, used the capsule for diabetic patients who wish to avoid the cane sugar and honey carriers.)

The powerful antioxidant combination of MAK-4 and MAK-5 is the only thing known that protects the body with the same efficiency as the three naturally occurring enzymes SOD, catalase, and glutathione peroxidase. MAK-4 and MAK-5 have been shown to neutralize the free radical damage produced when a potent anti-cancer drug (adriamycin) was given to both animals and humans. The two formulas reduced the death rate in animals by 60 percent.

When Dr. Stephen Bondy at the University of California-Irvine tested the Mak-4 formula against the toxic effects of toluene, a hazardous industrial solvent, he found that it effectively scavenged the free radicals that toluene creates.

I have used MAK-4 and MAK-5 in cancer patients for the last seven years with a great deal of confidence, knowing that it protects them against the side effects of chemotherapy and offers them an alternative way to deal with the progression of their disease. And, in fact, I believe that *all* patients with cancer and auto-immune diseases should be offered MAK-4 and MAK-5 in combination with high doses of vitamin C. For maximum free-radical protection, MAK-4 and MAK-5 should absolutely be part of your daily regimen.

**How much you should take:** I recommend one teaspoon of MAK-4 and one MAK-5 tablet twice a day. Individuals with heart disease, cancer, or immune-deficiency disorders should take two to four teaspoons of MAK-4 and two tablets of MAK-5 twice a day.

## The flavonoids

Albert Szent-Gyorgyi, M.D., Ph.D., received the Nobel Prize in 1937 for his discovery of vitamin C and flavonoids. He was the first to identify a flavonoid deficiency as one of the hallmarks of scurvy. These compounds were initially called "vitamin P" because of their ability to reduce blood vessel permeability.

The flavonoids have been known as "nature's biologic modifiers" because they have the ability to modify the body's reaction to compounds such as allergens, viruses, and substances that cause cancer. Much research is being done presently on the flavonoids for their use in the treatment of disease. Quercetin, for example, fights bacteria in the intestinal tract. Two citrus bioflavonoids, lutein and hesperidin, change capillary blood flow. And the flavonoids in green tea have been shown to help protect against cancer of the rectum, gall bladder, and endometrium.

**How much you should take:** In a nutshell, lots! Antioxidant flavonoids should be used extensively for health maintenance as well as during illness. You'll read more about getting these compounds in foods later in this chapter. But right now, for openers, you should be drinking two to three cups of green tea every day. If you're sensitive to caffeine, get the decaffeinated variety. If you don't like the taste, try one of the green teas that is blended with antioxidant herbs such as rosemary.

I also recommend grapeseed extract in a dose of one milligram per pound of body weight. You should also take Pycnogenol, a proprietary extract of pine bark, in an initial dose of two milligrams per pound of body weight for two to four weeks, and then one milligram per pound for maintenance. For my patients who have cancer, I double the dose of grapeseed extract and/or Pycnogenol.

### Alpha-lipoic acid

This compound plays a vital part in the body's energy-producing reactions. It is involved in the conversion of carbohydrates into energy.

**How much you should take:** I recommend 200 to 400 milligrams of oral alpha-lipoic acid per day for healthy individuals. There is evidence that this same dose is effective in enhancing the immune system in HIV-positive patients. For my patients with diabetes, I increase the dose to 800 to 1,200 milligrams.

Intravenous alpha-lipoic acid has been used recently in Germany in diabetics to offset the side effects of peripheral neuropathy. I have used intravenous alpha-lipoic acid in my diabetic patients with this painful condition in doses ranging from 600 to 1,200 milligrams per day. This is one situation in which I always make sure the patient is also taking at least 100 micrograms of selenium and high doses of vitamin E.

### Antioxidant spices

Black pepper, chili peppers, cumin, ginger, and turmeric all have very important antioxidant properties. I find that the use of black pepper along with liberal amounts of chili peppers and cumin is very helpful in the treatment of all inflammatory diseases of the joints (such as arthritis) and all autoimmune diseases (such as lupus). There is no toxic dose.

**How much you should take:** It is possible to take an extract of black pepper and chili pepper in capsule form, but there is no evidence that these products have any antioxidant benefits. Just buy these spices in their freshest form, in quantity, and use them liberally in cooking. For the best flavor, grind black pepper and cumin seed fresh when you use them. You can keep fresh ginger root in the freezer for a month and chop off a chunk when needed.

## Another source of antioxidants

In Chapter 10, we'll talk about how to change your diet for the maximum anti-aging effects. But in this chapter, now that you know about antioxidants, I want to tell you about how to furnish your body with naturally occurring antioxidant phytochemicals.

"Phyto" means plant. Phytochemicals are complex substances such as sulforaphane, present in broccoli, that actually sweep cancer-causing agents out of your cells. These phytochemicals naturally occur in some foods.

Intense study of phytochemicals has just begun, but already we have found benefits from some of them: the flavonoids in citrus fruits and berries, P-courmaric acid and cholorogenic acid in tomatoes, allicin in garlic and onions, capsaicin in chili peppers, and genistein in soybeans.

Eating vegetables, fruits, onions, and garlic wards off cancer by filling your body with disease fighters and free-radical neutralizers.

Fruits and vegetables also are high in fiber, so they help protect against colon cancer, breast cancer, and all types of intestinal cancer.

I advocate a diet high in freshly grown fruits, vegetables, and grains. This diet, similar to the diet eaten by our ancestors, will help give you additional antioxidant chemical protection.

Here are some examples of the beneficial phytochemicals you'll find in foods. You'll see that some of them are the same vitamins I'm recommending that you take in supplement form.

• Vitamin A. The best source of vitamin A is still cod liver oil. Other sources include beef liver, chili peppers, collard greens, and dandelions. After those foods come carrots, apricots, kale, sweet potatoes, parsley, and cantaloupe.

• Beta-carotene is present in most green plants but especially in sweet potatoes, carrots, squash, spinach, apricots, and green peppers.

• Lycopene, another very important antioxidant carotenoid, is present in tomatoes, carrots, green peppers, and apricots. Tomatoes are the best source.

• Lutein is found in green plants, spinach, carrots, and tomatoes.

• Vitamin C. While it is usually thought that oranges and other citrus fruits are the major source of vitamin C, red chili peppers, guava, red bell peppers, kale leaves, and parsley have three to four times the concentration of this super antioxidant of an orange. Exposure to air gradually destroys vitamin C. For example, a cucumber that is sliced and left standing loses 40 to 50 percent of its vitamin C within three hours. So for maximum vitamin C healing power, fix that salad fresh.

• Vitamin E. This potent antioxidant is found in wheat germ oil, seeds, nuts, and whole grains but also in asparagus, avocadoes, berries, green leafy vegetables, and tomatoes.

• Bioflavonoids are responsible for the colors of many fruits, flowers, and vegetables. They are found in grapefruit, oranges, apples, peaches, cranberries, cherries, grapes, plums, carrots, onions, parsley, rhubarb, dried beans, some green teas, red wine, and sage.

• Chromium, while not specifically thought to be an antioxidant, is the key constituent of the glucose tolerance factor that is very important in the aging process. Food sources of chromium include brewer's yeast, whole wheat bread, wheat bran, and rye bread.

• Selenium is present in wheat germ, brazil nuts, oats, whole wheat bread, and barley.

• Alpha-lipoic acid is a sulphur-containing vitamin-like substance that has now been shown to be a good antioxidant. Major sources of lipoic acid include liver and yeast, foods that are not commonly eaten.

• Coenzyme Q10. The best food sources of CoQ10 are plant-based foods. In fact, vegetarians usually have twice the level of CoQ10 in their bodies that omnivores do. This indicates that a high intake of plant foods may help preserve high CoQ10 levels.

You can see that if you want to protect yourself against the progressive aging process and live that healthy life at 100, you'll want to have a plant-based diet that contains maximum variety. You'll want to reduce free-radical injuries caused by exposure to sunlight, radiation, and chemicals.

## Rediscovering Healing Herbs

Herbal remedies have been used for centuries in other cultures, but have been generally ignored by the Western medical establishment. Recently, however, even the most conservative researchers have started to take note of the time-proven benefits of medicinal plants. Scientists are journeying into rain forests, to the Himalayas, to the Indian tribes of Peru to study ancient herbal treatments still used by "medicine men" and "shamans." Why? Because they work.

There are many beneficial herbs that can be used as food flavorings, in herbal teas, or in capsule, tincture, or freeze-dried doses. The following herbs are known to be high in antioxidant compounds: rosemary, lemon balm, thyme, oregano, sage, ginger, garlic, turmeric, and echinacea. Other spices believed by some experts to promote antioxidant activity include basil, allspice, lemon grass, mace, nutmeg, celery seed, black pepper, hot chili peppers, cloves, capsicum, cumin, and alfalfa leaves.

You also must realize that your body simply cannot protect you from all the free-radical injuries you will have. You'll want to provide it with foods that are high in antioxidants plus additional antioxidants in the form of supplements.

If you want to put antioxidants to work in your body—and I must say again that this is the second most important step (after aerobics) that you can take to promote your own health and to guarantee yourself good health to the age of 100—I urge you to start taking antioxidant supplements now.

In fact, if you take no other action as a result of reading this book, at least boost your antioxidant levels. You can't argue that taking some additional supplements takes up much of your time! But you will see almost immediate, visible, tangible evidence that these substances are working to protect you from free radical damage. Patients who take this advice report increased energy, positive changes in skin texture, and even loss of wrinkles—all within a few weeks.

And please, if you simply must smoke and eat fatty foods and continue other behaviors that promote free radical damage, at least be aware of the risks you run. Mitigate those risks as much as possible, not only by taking antioxidant vitamins and supplements, but by eating a diet rich in antioxidant vegetables (red, orange, and yellow) and herbs.

We are, today, on the leading edge of a new practice of medicine—21st century medicine. At last, the wisdom of the ancients, who have long known that plants hold healing power, has been combined with the modern technology developed by some of the world's greatest scientific minds. The result is that we're unlocking the keys to living long and healthy lives, lives that we can enjoy for every moment that we live them.

CHAPTER 7

# MANAGING STRESS

◆

*Imagine that when you're born, your skin is perfectly clean, smooth, and unwrinkled. Now imagine that every day, you have to take your hand and put it in a bucket of mud. Imagine how much mud you would have on your hand by the age of 20, 40, 50, or 70. Now think of all the negative physical and emotional influences that affect your life. These influences are like mud accumulating on your central nervous system. No wonder you get sick. You think you're taking care of your body—but your hand goes back in that bucket of mud every day.*

*The positive influences in your life are like a small pail of water that helps rinse off some of this mud. But what if you could cleanse your hand in a vast pool? What if eventually, you could cleanse it completely? That's what meditation can do.*

◆

I have often said that if there were one thing I wish I could leave as a legacy, it would be to teach every American the value of meditation. We all have stress in our lives, but depending on how you react to yours, this one chapter may be the most important one in this book to you. If I can convince you to start on a lifetime of meditation, you will reduce your risk of death and disease by much more than you will if you take antioxidants or change your diet.

I believe the central nervous system is something like a human radio antenna, and that it is directly affected by the conscious and unconscious messages we send it. Your antenna receives and processes thousands of stimuli every day from everything you see, smell, touch, taste, and feel. Peptides, hormones produced by your brain in response to these stimuli, travel through the spinal fluid, down the spinal column to the nerves and all the organs of your body.

Doctors and scientists who study the connections between psychology, neurology, the endocrine system and the nervous system have shown that thoughts and emotions create a chemical change in the brain. Depression, for example, is associated with a deficiency of the brain chemical serotonin, just one of the effects of too much stress.

## How stress causes disease

I believe these chemical changes—whether they are caused by a virus, an emotion, or a carcinogen—are the cause of disease. I believe that they can change cell chemistry in such a way that the cell's DNA receives a message to alter the way in which the cell functions. Cancer may begin at this cellular level, for example, or diabetes may occur.

In his book, *Human Physiology, Expression of Veda and the Vedic Literature*, Tony Nader, M.D., Ph.D., deals with this concept in a much more complicated way. In traditional Vedic literature, totality, or brahm, is equivalent to the individual human body. Dr. Nader has shown, in a very elaborate fashion, that the descending tracks of the central nervous system are associated with the structure of the human physiology, and that the cell nucleus, the major part of the cell that carries the DNA, is associated with enlightenment. In other words, the mind, the body, and the universe are interconnected. (This, by the way, is the basis upon which the Ayurvedic medical system was developed more than 5,000 years ago.)

## Symptoms of stress

When too many stimuli from the outside world bombard your central nervous system (the brain, spinal cord, and associated nerve endings), the result is an imbalance. This imbalance might manifest itself as symptoms of over-activity: your mind races, you have insomnia, and you can't relax. Eventually, your stomach, heart, and skin are affected. You might develop Crohn's disease, psoriasis, or irritable bowel syndrome.

Such overstimulation can also cause the opposite effect: you're always tired, you sleep too much, and you can't concentrate. Eventually, this can lead to chronic fatigue syndrome, slow circulation to the heart and other organs, platelet stickiness and heart attacks, heart disease, and constipation.

## The benefits of regular meditation

Scientifically, it is known that those who meditate regularly have less chronic illness, in general, and a decreased risk of dying from the major killers: heart disease and cancer. It has also been statistically shown that meditators spend fewer days in the hospital when they have an illness that requires surgical intervention. For example, if a patient who doesn't meditate has his gall bladder removed, he can expect an average hospital stay of four to five days, compared with half that time for a patient who meditates regularly.

When researchers use IGF-1 levels (an indirect measure of levels of human growth hormone) to calculate physiologic age, every year of regular meditation begins to reduce an individual's physiologic age by one half year. For example, if you began regular meditation at age 40, you would begin to see benefits by age 45 and by the age of 50, you would have the physiologic body of a 45-year-old.

It's well known that transcendental meditation (TM) guards against high blood pressure. But that's not all. In 1978, physiologist R. Keith Wallace, a researcher at the University of California at Los Angeles, discovered that even novice meditators experienced profound relaxation and significant changes in breathing, heartbeat, and blood pressure.

Wallace also proved that by practicing this form of meditation one year or more, blood pressure, the ability to see close, and hearing (three of the so-called "markers" of aging) all improved. In fact, his research showed that meditators who had been practicing TM for less than five years had a biological age five years younger than their chronological age—and those who had practiced TM for more than five years had an average biological age 12 years younger than their chronological age.

In addition, he discovered that meditators visited doctors and entered hospitals only half as often as those in a control group, and that they experienced 80 percent less heart disease and more than 50 percent less cancer than those in the control group.

However, there are many other forms of meditation that have the same benefits. Those individuals who practice centering prayer, for example, gain just as much as those who practice TM.

Some people avoid transcendental meditation or other forms of relaxation therapy because they have the mistaken idea that these practices are "religious" and may go against their own beliefs, whatever those might be.

To be sure, in some cultures, meditation is part of the practice of religion (in Zen Buddhism, for example). However, just as not all religions include the formal practice of meditation, not all meditation is religious. To put your mind at ease about this point, note that when you meditate, you can focus on any phrase or image.

If you want to live a healthy life at 100, you must practice meditation on a daily basis in order to dissipate the inescapable stress that is part of life. Many of my patients routinely thank me for enlightening them about meditation and say it's the single item in my program that has had the most profound impact on their lives.

## Knowing the enemy

Stress is one of the causes of high blood pressure, the so-called "silent killer" that's a root cause of heart attack, stroke, and even kidney failure. Stress is a contributing factor in ulcers and has been pointed to as a possible cause for immune-system weakness. Some research indicates that in a worst-case scenario—that is, if you're a so-called "hot reactor," and sudden stress causes a surge of adrenaline and epinephrine to hit your heart—stress can lead to sudden death.

Even if you're not a hot reactor, stress can make your life miserable. It can lead to blinding headaches, stomach upset, and debilitating back pain. It can make you lash out at loved ones and co-workers. Long-term stress causes mental anguish and can irreparably damage careers and relationships.

One study showed that a remarkable 85 percent of all visits to primary care physicians are for stress-related illnesses. A second study, a recent survey by Northwestern National Life Insurance of Minneapolis, Minnesota, measured job-related stress and showed that almost half the workers surveyed experienced job-related stress in 1991 (the year of the survey). It showed that about 65 percent had suffered exhaustion, anger, anxiety, or muscle pain due to stress, and that 72 percent experienced three or more stress-related illnesses in the year prior to the survey.

Stress is, according to many experts, the most common disease of our age. Millions of men and women complain of feeling "stressed out" by their jobs, by family pressures, or simply by life in a world seemingly filled with stressors. These are the men and women who shake their fists and curse at other drivers on the crowded interstate, who scream at co-workers over slight misunderstandings, or who sit silently at their desks being eaten alive by their own unresolved anger—and who die red-faced and gasping because they couldn't find a parking space.

I always feel a sense of sadness and frustration when I see people being literally robbed of life by stress. My heart goes out to them because I know from experience how easy it is to deal with stress in a positive way. How easy it is for anyone to safely manage any stressful situation.

By learning stress management, you can turn a would-be negative into a positive. By learning to deal with your stress, you will become a stronger person. You will be more resilient. You will interact with your spouse and your children in positive ways. You will begin to work better and to be more productive. You will enjoy your leisure time more fully, loving the moment and not fretting about either the past or the future. All because you learned how to deal with stress in positive ways.

## Stress management has to be learned

I said stress management was easy—not that it was something we're born with. Stress management must be learned. It's not something that comes naturally to most people. That's why so many medical centers, corporations, large and small businesses, organizations, and professional groups sponsor stress management classes or seminars. And that's why I decided to make stress management an integral part of my program to a century of great health.

During the past 20 years, I have helped thousands of patients cope with stress and have spoken to hundreds of professional groups about stress management. I have met with stressed executives, managers, physicians, dentists, and others. Through this, I have gained insights into what causes stress, how to manage stress—and even how to use some stress in positive ways. It's important to know as much as you can about how stress works, and how it works in you.

## Physical stress and emotional stress

Physical stress is easy to understand. If you run up three flights of stairs, the physical stress on your body is immediate and easy to recognize. Depending on the shape you're in, that exercise could cause a slight burning in your thigh muscles—or it could make your leg muscles ache and knot, your heart pound, and your chest heave as you gasp for breath.

Your body's reaction to sudden emotional stress is also immediate and easy to recognize. If, for example, you're driving along a road late at night and a deer leaps in front of your car, your body will react instantly. As you slam on the brakes, your mouth will go dry, your pulse will quicken,

## Too Hot To Cool Down

The "hot reactor" was first clinically described by Robert Elliot, M.D. When I first read about Dr. Elliot's research I was skeptical. His research described a type of person in whom a negative reaction to stress can lead to sudden death. These individuals are subject to long-term wear and tear, but show few symptoms of it. Then, due to some stimulus that may even be minor, they get a sudden jolt of adrenaline—a jolt so strong that it literally destroys the heart muscle. Medical science once thought the cause of death in these cases was heart attack, but it is now widely accepted that stress itself is the cause.

There are hot reactors who have the stereotypical type A personalities—harddriving executive types who never take the time to relax, who eat too much of the wrong food, who smoke and drink, and who appear to be ideal candidates for sudden death due to stress. Then there are hot reactors who are type B personalities— easy-going, laid-back, seemingly always in control.

Personality has nothing to do with whether a person is a hot reactor. The term refers only to the way a person's body reacts to stress. His blood pressure will jump without any symptoms of heart disease, and his cardiac output (the amount of blood that flows from and your breathing will become ragged.

Other forms of stress are less obvious. You can, for example, experience some stress if you have to make a difficult decision and spend days, or even weeks, agonizing over a course of action that might have serious consequences.

the heart) will drop—thus making the ultimate stress-related heart injury possible.

In 1984, I had an experience with a 42-year-old male that made me a believer in hot reactors. Before his death, this patient was in relatively good health. He had some problems that seemed to be associated with a decision he had made in 1983 to start his own business, but those problems were minor.

He had gained weight, he had more head colds than usual, he had developed a skin rash, and he found himself getting irritable with his children and losing interest in family affairs. He had a normal insurance physical in 1983 and a normal general physical in early 1984. Both of those exams disclosed no heart anomalies. And yet, late that year, he was found dead in his kitchen, where he'd gone to prepare breakfast.

An autopsy showed that while the blood vessels leading to his heart were normal, the damage that had been done to his heart muscle was the type of damage usually associated with the sudden blockage of an artery.

This sudden blockage is exactly what Elliot and others have shown is the result of a sudden stress-related jolt of adrenaline in the body.

The good news for hot reactors is that they can protect themselves by using stress management techniques and by taking prescribed medication, if that is indicated.

You might experience great stress if you're working on a major project for a difficult boss, laboring under the knowledge that your performance could literally make or break your career. Even preparations for a happy event can create stress—the marriage of your daughter, a long-delayed European vacation, the purchase of the 36-foot sloop you always wanted.

In every case, stress is related to an event or chain of events. It doesn't just appear from nowhere.

## Stress is always with you

You can't eliminate all the stressors in your life. Deer are going to leap in front of your car. You're going to have to deal with difficult employers, employees, and relatives. Difficult business decisions and personal decisions will crop up. And there are some stressors that you wouldn't want to eliminate even if you could—cheering your son through a championship soccer game, for example, or having to make a speech after you've won the Nobel Prize!

The secret of stress management is not eliminating stressors, but changing the way you react to them. Just as you can physically condition yourself to run up three flights of stairs without physical stress, so can you mentally condition yourself to deal with the stressful situations in your life.

## Your stress is uniquely yours

Before you can begin to change the way you react to stress, you must first identify the things in your own life that produce stress.

It seems that this should be easy, but it's not. There's no

set formula here. Something that creates stress for one man or woman may not be stressful—and may even be pleasant—to another. In fact, studies conducted several years ago to test the stress-adaptability of test pilots working for the U.S. Department of Defense showed just how personal this matter truly is.

In these tests, it was discovered that pilots were actually comfortable in situations in which they were in great danger—at times when the average person would expect to be paralyzed by fear. Many of these same pilots, though, hit uncomfortable stress levels when faced with some situations that many of us deal with comfortably on a day-to-day basis—like a room full of preschoolers. Everyone has a different "comfort zone."

In their book *The C Zone*, researchers Robert Kriegel, M.D., and Marilyn Kriegel, M.D., say that there is a zone where each individual is comfortable with the amount of stress he or she is experiencing. There is also a zone of distress where the same individual is uncomfortable. The Kriegels say these zones are different for each individual.

Some people, for example, find that speaking in public is an exhilarating experience. The natural nervousness associated with the experience of delivering a speech in public is experienced by these individuals as a positive, and they perform better because of it. Other men and women are simply terrified at the prospect of public speaking. They have a negative, destructive reaction to this stress and may experience nausea, memory lapses, or worse if forced to perform before strangers.

## Recognize your body's signals

Because of the personal nature of stress, I obviously

can't give you a list of specific things that will cause you stress and then tell you how to deal with each of those in turn. I can, however, explain how you can begin to recognize your own stressors.

Most of us know when we are experiencing stress, though we may not recognize it by that name. But we know we're experiencing something that makes us uncomfortable or uneasy. That's because our physiology undergoes changes when we're faced with a stressful situation. Like all members of the animal kingdom, when you are placed in a situation that you perceive to be dangerous or fearful, your body reacts immediately, pushing you to choose between "fight or flight."

According to researchers, here are just a few of the things that happen as your body prepares to take action:

• Your brain processes your emotions and creates certain peptides, or protein-like substances, which then send a signal to the adrenal glands, as well as the other hormone-producing glands such as the thyroid, pancreas, and pituitary.

• The adrenal glands respond to those peptides and start to produce adrenaline. This hormone makes your heart beat faster and harder and elevates your blood pressure.

• Your adrenal glands also excrete cortisone that shuts down the nervous system functions that would otherwise calm the fight or flight response. However, because cortisone is part of your body's immune mechanism, pumping out lots of it in times of stress can reduce your resistance to infection. Excess cortisone can also reduce your stomach's resistance to acid and lead to ulcers and colon problems, including Crohn's disease and irritable bowel syndrome.

• Your thyroid gland starts to make its hormones, T-3 and T-4. These hormones speed up your metabolism and can contribute to jitteriness, nervousness, or insomnia.

• Your blood sugar rises in response to the cortisone to give you an initial burst of energy. In response, your pancreas starts to produce insulin to process the increased sugar. Overworking your pancreas can lead to an abnormal metabolic response, one that can cause the sugar to be burned too fast or be stored as fat. You can even wear out the pancreas. After overproducing insulin for a long period of time, your pancreas begins to malfunction, your blood sugar fluctuates between high and low—and you eventually develop diabetes.

• Your liver starts to pump out cholesterol to provide your body with fuel. Because of too much cholesterol in circulation, your blood platelets start to get sticky in preparation to plug up whatever injuries you might receive. Over time, these sticky platelets can plug up a blood vessel and you could have a heart attack or stroke.

## All this because of one stimulus

All of these changes in your body occur at high speed as the result of just one thought or one abnormal stimulus. Just because one jerk cut you off in traffic, or the cable reception went out at a critical point in your favorite TV show, or your boss ignored your hard work to praise a co-worker.

The easiest way for you to determine that you're experiencing stress is to pay attention to your body's signals and learn to recognize when you're in this fight or flight mode, so you can do something about it before the stress starts to damage your body.

You can't walk around with a blood pressure cuff on all the time, but you can watch for dry throat, headache, upset stomach, pain in the neck or lower back, heart palpitations, and rapid breathing. Signs of longer-term stress may include shortness of temper, a lack of interest in hobbies and pastimes you typically enjoy, a lack of the desire to spend time with your family members or loved ones, sleeplessness, a lack of sexual desire, the loss of appetite, and fatigue in the morning.

## Soul searching about stress

Before I tell you about three techniques to keep stress from damaging your body, I want to show you some ways to actually reduce stress at its source. I can't buy your boss a sense of humor or send your children to spend their difficult adolescences (or their midlife crises) in Europe. But I can show you some ways to think about sources of stress creatively.

Obviously, there are some truly dangerous situations that you might have to face in which physically fighting or fleeing are, literally, your only options. If, for example, you wake up to the blaring of your smoke alarm, your body will get you geared up to gather the family and run for your life. And you wouldn't want it to do anything else!

However, in most stressful situations, when our bodies are telling us to either bolt or do battle, neither of these options is truly appropriate. Instead, we usually react by either flying into a rage or internalizing our fear and anger—doing damage to ourselves in the process.

## Understanding the stressor

In general, stress originates with some sort of conflict. The greater the conflict, the greater the imbalance—and, ultimately, the greater the stress.

Your stress may stem from a conflict with another person, or from a conflict with the rules of an impersonal organization or institution. You may also have an inner conflict if your actions or situation are not in agreement with your values or true beliefs, if you're not living your life the way you want to or in a way that you find admirable or worthwhile.

Stress management doesn't focus on changing the situation. It focuses on how to turn a negative, destructive reaction into one that is positive. Perhaps you're stressed because you have a demanding boss who wants everything done his way—even though you completely disagree with him. No matter how hard you try, he makes you feel threatened and afraid of losing your job.

What if you were able to believe in the idea that while your demanding boss may not know as much as you do about some things, he's still your boss. And as long as he signs your paycheck, he doesn't have much of an incentive to change his mind about how things should be done. Once you realize that you can't change him, you might decide that your best course of action is to agree and simply earn that paycheck. Wouldn't that de-stress your interaction with your boss? What if, when you tried things his way without telling yourself in your head how "wrong and unfair" it was, his way turned out to work better?

What if you were to view the loss of your job not as a financial disaster, but as an opportunity to find a better job, to grow, and possibly make more money? Wouldn't that make you feel less stressed in interactions with this boss?

Or perhaps you're stressed because you are working from dawn to dusk, day after day, forced by your need to succeed or to make money into spending too much time at the office when you'd rather spend that time with your family. Not only are you in conflict with yourself here (you're not doing what you really want to do), but your stress may be compounded because you're afraid you're losing your family's love.

In such situations, you need to be able to analyze the reasons for your stress. For example, in your decision to work 80 hours a week, the root cause of your stress is the conflict between your values and your actions. In conflict

## How One Man Faced the Unfaceable

While reading the *Sun Sentinel* today, I was struck by an article written by one of my favorite columnists, Ray Reechi. His column had not appeared for the last few weeks, and, today, he apologized by saying, "I weighed the pros and cons of sharing this information with my readers. On the one hand, most people have enough troubles without being burdened with mine. On the other hand, this column has always been very personal."

Ray went on to write that his doctors had found cancer in his pancreas and liver. How could he see a positive side to that?

In his words, "I found out how many people really care about me. And I don't mean just my closest friends and acquaintances. The outpouring of care and concern has touched me more than once."

between a micromanaging boss and your own initiative, perhaps the real cause of stress is your inability to use your own creativity at that particular job or profession.

Once you understand why you're stressed, you'll be able to take action to do something about it. You might choose to switch to a less-demanding job—or tell your bosses it's time to expand their workforce so you can cut back on your hours. Or you might negotiate limits on the long hours, and make sure that there are specific rewards for them—rewards that you can share with your family.

Whatever your course of action, you can eliminate or at least minimize stress by examining the conflict, finding its root—and ending it by changing the way you look at the situation.

He went on to say that he had never been tested before. He had never been called to war or put in any real life-threatening situations. "Now I know," he said, "and it's good to know."

A friend had asked Ray if he wasn't tempted to ask, "Why me?" He responded, "Sure. A little. But I'm just as tempted to ask, 'Why not me?' Besides, that's all wasted energy. I'd rather use my strength to fight this thing."

Ray wrote that he realized that fighting his illness would not leave him with a lot of energy to write very much in the near future. But, he said, "I plan to try any time I feel well enough. So I'll thank you in advance for your prayers and good wishes, and hope to be back on these pages regularly and soon."

Like Ray, by owning your problems, you empower yourself to stop wasting time and energy trying to change those people, institutions, or situations that cause you stress. Such time and energy is usually wasted.

## But first you have to take charge

Each of us has the power to control our own reactions to stress and to determine if those reactions will have a positive or negative effect on us.

This is why, in the several hundred stress management talks I've given to professional groups over the years and in my work teaching my patients how to use the tools of stress management, one of the first things I do is to drive home the point that we each have to "own" our own problems. You are not stressed by "him" or by "that thing" or by "those events." It's your reactions that cause you stress.

This doesn't mean that "he" didn't screw up and "that thing" isn't terrible and "those people" haven't hurt you. Life is unfair and unpredictable. But it does mean that, because the reactions that are damaging you are yours, only you can change them. And you have to take the responsibility to change them.

## How knowing your priorities helps

Once you've taken the responsibility for dealing with your own stress, you need to have a clear understanding of what's really important to you before you can take action to eliminate the conflicts in your life. It's when reality or our own actions violates these important values that conflict occurs.

Start by making a list of your priorities. Relax with your eyes closed for a few moments. Then, open your eyes and list the things that are important to you, in descending order of importance. Your list might look something like this:

GOD
FAMILY
  Wife
  Children
  Parents
  In-Laws
WORK
  Career goals
  Job relationships
  Current projects
HEALTH
  Staying well
  Fighting disease
MONEY
  Managing on a daily basis
  Investment objectives
RELATIONSHIPS

Then, after relaxing for a few more moments, answer the following questions:
- What do I most like to do?
- What do I least like to do?
- What do I wish I could do that I don't or won't do?
- What qualities do I admire most in other people?
- What qualities do I dislike in others?

This simple self-examination will give you a good idea of what your priorities are. By concentrating on these priorities, you'll be able to identify the root cause of the stress generated by a specific situation. Then you'll be able to defuse the stress by understanding how you need to change your perception of that situation in order to get rid of the conflict.

## Three ways to manage stress

Any form of stress management that you use will make you healthier and happier. You'll be healthier because you'll be intervening in or stopping the wear-and-tear process that leads to so much illness. And you'll be happier because you'll feel better and you'll no longer be reacting inappropriately to the conflicts in your life. You'll no longer be causing rifts between yourself and your loved ones. Instead, your actions and your beliefs will be in harmony. You will be living a life that is truly worthwhile.

But you'll need three specific techniques to effectively manage all of the different kinds of stress in your life. They are: regular, preferably daily, relaxation therapy (such as transcendental meditation); stress intervention techniques that use your senses to counter acute stress when it happens; and physical activity to dissipate stress hormones.

We've already discussed the benefits of aerobic exercise in chapter 5. But one of the most important reasons to exercise aerobically is that stress triggers the release of certain hormones in your body. Elevated levels of these hormones can be destructive. And the importance of lowering these elevated hormonal levels through exercise can't be overstated.

In fact, all the relaxation therapy in the world, coupled with acute intervention, is much, much less effective if it is not coupled with hormonal stress reduction through exercise. Though any type of activity will work, the best activity for this purpose is aerobic exercise in which you elevate your pulse rate to a predetermined level.

There are many forms of physical activity that will help relieve stress. Gardening, playing tennis, racquetball, golf, flying an airplane, sky diving, going for a long walk, and lifting weights—all have similar benefits in increasing endorphins.

In addition, as you exercise and your heart, lungs, and circulatory systems improve, a chain reaction of health improvements will occur. Nutrients and oxygen will move more easily to all parts of your body, which means that wastes will be more easily removed and your enzyme system will be in better balance, which means that your muscles will relax more completely. You'll sleep better, your endurance will increase, and you'll have more fun.

## Acute stress intervention

In addition to exercise, you need a technique that you can use during sudden instances of heightened stress. Obviously, you can't stop a business meeting that's going badly or an argument with your spouse for 10 minutes of meditation. So, you need to know what to do when you realize that you're under acute stress. And you might need to use it tomorrow!

Acute stress intervention techniques use your five senses—sight, smell, hearing, taste, and touch—to instantly slow the progression of stress reactions in your body.

One of the best ways to release tension is to laugh. Many people—including me—find that something as simple and silly as a child's wind-up toy gives them the laugh break they need when they are stressed out.

Now, you can't always meditate and you can't always pull a wind-up toy from your pocket or purse. But there are things you can do that have the same end result. The secret here is to use your senses to calm you down. For example, perhaps you have a favorite painting, or a piece of music you love. Visualize that painting or listen to that melody in your head for a moment, and let your mind wander, recalling a relaxed, happy time.

This type of acute intervention technique is an excellent way to dissipate the physical effects of stress, and you can use it even in the middle of a business meeting or in a crowded, snowed-in airport. It works because it is very difficult to feel worry, fear, anger, or resentment when you're visualizing pleasant sights and sounds. By taking a brief moment to tune out and calm down, you will be able to refocus on the important issues that you have to deal with.

When used long-term, the regular practice of sensory stress intervention will help raise your stress threshold. In other words, it will take more stress to push you to the point where you're feeling angry or fearful.

## What relaxation therapy can do

When you practice relaxation therapy every day, you dissipate some of the negative effects of stressors. When I talk about relaxation therapy, I'm referring to this technique's many forms, including listening to music in a quiet place, sitting and thinking mindful thoughts, praying—any technique that allows you to dissipate the negative effects of stress on your body. Self-hypnosis and imagery, guided or not, are some of my favorite ways to practice the relaxation response.

But there are differences between these forms of relaxation therapy that you should be aware of. Meditation rejuvenates your self-healing mechanisms and cleans the debris of past stress from the central nervous system. But the only benefit of other relaxation therapies is that they neutralize some of the end results of too much cortisone and too much blood sugar on the organs of the body.

## Taking a tip from kids

One of my mentors, George Sheehan, M.D., taught me the importance of learning how to play as if I were a five-year-old child again. That was my inspiration for creating an acute intervention technique that I continue to use today—what I call my wind-up-toy technique of stress management.

You know what I mean by a wind-up toy—those little one- and two-dollar gizmos that you find in just about every convenience store, drug store, and supermarket. Well, I have a whole collection of them. In fact, many of my patients bring me wind-up toys as gifts whenever they run across one that's especially cute. My current favorites are a little alligator that opens and closes its snout when it's wound up, and a monkey that does flips. I keep these toys on my desk, and when the stresses of my day get to me, I wind one up and watch it. This never fails to make me smile. It's actually a form of biofeedback—a signal to me that says, "Lighten up, Bob!"

Obviously, when I'm in an important meeting and some jerk starts putting me under pressure, I can't take out one of my wind-up toys and put it on the table (although, on occasion, I have thought of doing just that). What I do instead, is visualize the jerk as one of my wind-up toys. I might picture him opening and closing his alligator snout, or flipping like my monkey—anything that gives me a private little chuckle.

This technique is extremely beneficial because it affects almost all of my senses. For one thing, I have to wind up (touch) the toy. It has motion, so I watch it. It makes a clicking or snapping sound, so I listen to it. And, of course, when I laugh, I experience the physical change caused by bringing in more oxygen and expelling more carbon dioxide.

Meditation is a trained response that has to be learned. There are meditative states in Zen Buddhism, tai chi, yoga, and Ayurvedic medicine. The form of meditation that was popularized by the Beatles is transcendental meditation (TM). The reason I favor a technique like TM is that it allows you to use a mindless mantra to substitute for meaningful thoughts. A simple prayer, when it is repeated, is just as effective as a mantra, as long as you understand that the purpose of the prayer is to be a meaningless mantra.

If you don't want to use a mantra, you can use just about any phrase—a prayer such as "Jesus is my leader," for example, or "I want universal peace." Or a Native American chant. Or a Gregorian chant. Anything that allows you to dwell on the phrase itself, not its meaning. Some meditators use "shri namah," which, roughly translated from the Sanskrit, means "oh most beautiful I bow down." For the average individual, however, it is a meaningless phrase, and that's what makes it beneficial. You can use anything that allows you to dwell on the vibration of your breath, not on the meaning of the words.

However, TM is not something that you can learn to do by reading a book. You need to take formal instruction. At some point, you may wish to take that step.

## Learning focused meditation

For now, though, I'll teach you an alternative form of meditation that is very effective for stress management. I call this "focused meditation" because you relax by focusing your mind on an image, a sound, a word—anything that allows mind-body stress reduction.

Look at a clock to check your starting time. You should

keep your session to between 10 and 20 minutes.

1. Sit in a chair or on the floor, in any way that's comfortable for you.

2. Close your eyes.

3. Allow thoughts to enter your mind unbidden. Do not try to prevent thoughts. Do not try to "force" specific thoughts.

4. If you want to think about something that enters your mind, you can. Or you can just let it go and allow the next thought to enter.

5. After one to three minutes, gently open your eyes for 10 to 30 seconds.

6. Close your eyes again.

7. Let your thoughts flow. If you have pleasant thoughts, that's fine. If your thoughts are troubled, don't fight them. Keep your eyes closed and your mind open for one to three minutes. Open your eyes for about 30 seconds.

8. Close your eyes and concentrate on a pleasant image or place you know of or can imagine. Or repeat a calming word or phrase over and over and over again in your mind. Some people use words like "peace" or phrases such as "I am more relaxed" or "I feel calm" or even a prayer like "I love the Lord." If thoughts enter your mind, allow them to come in. But as soon as it's comfortable, reintroduce the phrase or image that you were focusing on before.

9. Continue to meditate for 10 to 20 minutes. Don't worry about the time. You can open one eye to glance briefly at a clock without interrupting your meditative state.

10. When the 10 to 20 minutes have passed, gently stretch, and then slowly open your eyes. Sit quietly for a minute or two before resuming your regular activities with renewed energy.

If, as some people report, you feel slightly fatigued when you finish your meditation, simply close your eyes for a few more minutes to relieve that fatigue and let energy flow through your body.

After you have been using focused meditation for 30 to 60 days, you may eliminate the steps where you open your eyes. Start with your eyes closed at the beginning of your session, and don't open them again until the end.

## Tips for better focused meditation

Do not try to meditate in bed or in a completely dark room. You don't want to confuse meditation with sleep. Meditate at least 90 minutes before bedtime. While meditation is cleansing to your central nervous system, it will give you energy and might make sleep difficult.

I believe you should meditate twice, not once, a day for an average of 20 minutes: once before you exercise or have breakfast, and the second time at the end of your work day before your evening meal. The first session will prepare you for the day's stressors, and the second will relieve you of the stressors you have encountered during that day.

Don't meditate lying down. You may play some soothing music while meditating, but don't set an alarm or allow any stimulus that could jolt you out of the meditative state, because interrupted meditation can be very irritating to your central nervous system.

Perhaps most important is for you not to become com-

pulsive about meditation. Enjoy it. While the most beneficial way to meditate is once in the morning and once in
the evening, it has been shown that regularity is more important than the amount of time spent. In other words, it's
better to meditate once a day each and every day, than to
randomly meditate twice in one day.

Hundreds of thousands of people meditate each day,
and the results they describe (the same results I've experienced from my own practice of TM for about 20 minutes
each morning and evening) are remarkable. Though I have
learned four or five other forms of meditation, this is the
most rewarding one for me. I also begin each of my meditation sessions with two or three minutes of prayer.

## What new meditators say:

There are three responses that I hear from my patients
when they begin to meditate:
• "I can't sit still long enough to use my mantra (or centering prayer or phrase)." I tell them to continue meditating. Even it they feel edgy and agitated, they are still getting some benefit.

• "I feel like I'm falling asleep." I tell them that this simply
means their central nervous system needs more rest. They
should continue to meditate and accept sleep if it comes.

• "I find a place that is both nurturing and incredibly rewarding. I have no sense of time or space, but I have a
sense of a higher level of awareness of the universe as a
whole." That's it! This is what we call the transcendent
state into the fourth level of consciousness.

## Remember the practice of patience

Meanwhile, as always, remember to be patient with yourself. Love yourself. Laugh a lot. Play a lot. Meditation is something that you're doing to help your health; it shouldn't cause stress in and of itself! Keep in mind that stress is the number-one cause of disease in the United States. Your three-part stress reduction plan—exercise, acute intervention, and regular meditation or relaxation therapy—will give you better health and quality of life to share with those you love.

Prayer connects me with my universal power—with my God. It is prayer that brings me peace, my best form of stress management. I urge you to continue your quest for your best form of stress management. And please keep me in your prayers—I will always keep you in mine.

# CHAPTER 8

# STRENGTH TRAINING

———— ✦ ————

*Your muscles have a choice between two futures. In one future, you carry a heavy potted plant without breathing hard. You reach the highest shelf in your closet and lift down that box of books you haven't seen in five years. You play with your grandkids (or great-grandkids) without getting worn out, and you win more tennis matches and drive tee shots closer to the green. You have lots of energy for work, play, sex—for the business and pleasure of everyday living.*

*In the other future, by the time you reach age 75, you're among the 65 percent of American women or the 25 percent of American men who can't lift anything heavier than 10 pounds. Which future would you choose?*

———— ✦ ————

In other words, when it comes to your muscles, it's a clear case of "use it or lose it!" And the earlier you choose to use your muscles in a weight-training program, the better off your overall health will be.

Why is this? Muscle cells that are well-conditioned—the kind of cells you had when you were an active young boy or girl—can contract to about half of their resting length and support more than a thousand times their own weight. But if you don't exercise, this ability diminishes as you age, and it starts diminishing as early as age 30. By the time you're 65, you will have lost from 30 to 40 percent of your strength and about 12 percent of your muscle mass.

But simple, moderate weight training can stop this loss of muscle, rebuild muscle, and provide lots of other benefits as well. It's proven, it's speedy, it's safe, and I can guarantee that, if you include weight training as part of a total program that also includes aerobics and healthy eating, you'll love the results.

How does weight training work? By increasing your muscle mass. The more muscle mass you have, the stronger you are. Balanced exercise that improves both strength and flexibility pairs what Eastern philosophies call "yang" energy, the energy of strength, with the "yin" energy of suppleness, which you'll read more about in the next chapter. What such philosophies would advise is that you need both strength and flexibility for truly balanced health.

Muscle mass is built by the repeated contractions of muscle fibers against medium to high resistance. Inside the body, such exercise depletes the muscle's enzymes and breaks down muscle fibers. When the muscle fibers rebuild themselves, they rebuild stronger, as if to say, "Take THAT!" to the rest of your body. In other words, the simple action of putting your muscles to work lifting moderate weights makes your muscles increase in size. And this happens no matter how old you are when you begin weight training.

You'll be able to see this process happening with your own eyes in a few months. You'll start feeling stronger within two weeks, and within three months, you'll double, or maybe even triple, your strength. What's more, fat will seem to drop off your body. The muscle mass that you've lost over the years will begin to reappear. Those embarrassing underarm "wattles" will be replaced by firm tissue. Your sagging chest will lift and shape.

## Invisible but crucial benefits

What you'll like even more are the benefits you can't see, but can feel.

**Less fat without dieting.** As your muscle mass increases, your metabolic rate speeds up, and that means you burn extra calories. Muscle requires more calories than fat to sustain itself. Your new, lean muscle mass will consume energy 24 hours a day, even if you're just relaxing. Pound for pound, muscle burns 40 to 50 more calories per day than fat. So, if you replace just five pounds of fat with five pounds of lean muscle, you'll burn off an additional 200 to 250 calories per day—even while you're sleeping.

This means that once you start weight training, you'll be able to eat more without gaining unwanted pounds—or that you'll be able to shed pounds without having to cut way back on your caloric intake.

**Decreased disease risk.** Another benefit of increased muscle mass is that it decreases your risk of diabetes. As the percentage of muscle mass in your body increases, your body requires less insulin to get sugar, or glucose, out of your blood and into your tissues, where it's required for energy. This means that your body is less likely to experience a shortage of insulin, making it less likely that you'll develop what's commonly called "adult-onset" diabetes.

Increased resistance to illness. The body's muscles are its main reservoirs for protein. Whenever you are sick, injured, under stress, or recovering from surgery, the body taps these reserves. So the stronger your muscles, the more protein you'll have available for your body in times of heightened need.

**Better cholesterol numbers.** Weight training increases the ratio of so-called "good" cholesterol, HDL, to "bad" cholesterol, LDL. That means a reduced risk of heart disease.

**Arthritis pain relief.** According to a study conducted by scientists at Tufts University, weight training may even help lessen the pain of both rheumatoid and progressive osteoarthritis. While the scientific jury is still out on this claim, apparently the "burn"—that uncomfortable warm feeling in the muscles that accompanies weight training—lessens the discomfort associated with arthritis. At the same time, weight training strengthens the muscles, tendons, and ligaments around joints, easing joint stress and, hence, easing arthritis-associated pain.

**Better bone strength.** Perhaps the most important benefit of weight training, however, is its ability to add bone density and actually replace bone cells that have been lost as part of the aging process. Researchers have discovered bones and connective tissues react much the same way that muscles do when challenged by weights or resistance: they grow stronger.

Bone weakness can lead to seemingly spontaneous fractures—the kind that occur when an older man or woman breaks a hip simply by stepping off a curb. And far too many out-of-shape senior citizens sustain fractures by stumbling, tripping, or falling while walking. These may seem like minor problems until you stop to think that such fractures are the leading cause of hospitalization for older Americans. For many of them, the result is a significant decrease in quality of life.

That's why weight training is particularly important for

## If You Have Heart Disease or High Blood Pressure

If you have either of these disorders, for you, flexibility is of paramount importance, and you should incorporate flexibility training (Chapter 9) into your health program first.

Still, you can (and should) embark on a weight-training program. For you, however, it's even more important to work with a professional trainer, preferably one with experience with people with heart or circulatory problems. You should also double the length of time you use the beginning phase of my program to 24 weeks.

older post-menopausal women who find themselves facing osteoporosis.

**Smarter aging.** Weight training even helps ward off senility, according to a study at Scripps College in Claremont, California. That study showed that men and women who exercise regularly perform better than sedentary people in reasoning, reaction times, and memory tests.

## How quickly weight training works

One of the great things about weight training is that it has nearly immediate results. You won't achieve anything like your full potential right away, to be sure. But you will, within just a few short weeks, notice changes in your body and in the way you feel and act—no matter how old you are when you start. But don't just take my word for it.

Take a peek at some of the research:

• One study focused on a group of 90-year-old women in Boston's Hebrew Rehabilitation Center for the Aged. This study showed that when the women were involved in a weight-training program for just eight weeks, they almost tripled their strength and added significantly to their muscle mass.

• Another study, this one at Tufts University's research center on aging, tracked a dozen men age 60 to 72 as they took part in a training program using a machine designed to strengthen leg muscles. After just three months of three sessions weekly, the muscle mass in the men's legs had increased significantly. Their extensor muscles (those that straighten the knee) were, on the average, 107 percent stronger. And strength in their flexor muscles (those that bend the joint) were, on average, 226 percent stronger.

• Researchers at McMaster University in Ontario proved that upper body strength can be quickly increased when they enrolled 14 men aged 60 to 70 in a 12-week program. The men exercised only one arm. When the study ended, lifting strength in the trained arms had increased an average of 48 percent, while strength in the untrained arms remained unchanged.

For all these reasons—plus the fact that strength training makes you feel healthier, stronger, and much more in control of your life—I advise virtually all my patients who to get involved in weight training along with aerobics and a healthy diet. And that's why I made weight training such an integral part of my program for a century or more of great health.

That's also why I was so pleased when the American College of Sports Medicine (ACSM), a professional organization of exercise experts of which I am a fellow, recently changed its "official prescription" for good health to include (for the first time ever) sessions of "moderate intensity" weight training with barbells, weight-bearing calisthenics, or resistance training machines. According to the ACSM, such a routine is a necessary part of any health program either for overall fitness or for a more active and agile old age.

Scientific evidence and my own experience with my patients has proved to me, beyond any shadow of a doubt, the many benefits of weight-training programs.

## It's not your dad's weight-training program

The days are gone when weight training meant making three weekly trips to a dank, dark gym where some heavyweight in a black t-shirt would put you through your paces using barbells and dumbbells.

These days, you can work out at home, using a variety of machines or "free weights" (barbells and dumbbells). Or you can join one of the new generation of health clubs where professional trainers will help you exercise using the very latest in strength-training equipment. Today's weight training goes by many names, including resistance training and strength training. The scientific name for this process is "isotonic training." That's just a fancy way of saying that the process involves making specific muscles in different parts of your body work harder than usual by pitting them against a resistance—the weight.

You can easily tailor a weight-training program to meet your schedule, your budget, and your personal taste. No matter how busy you are, you can fit weight training into your life. In fact, if you follow my recommendation—namely to exercise the major muscle groups in moderation at least twice weekly and preferably three times weekly—you'll spend only one to two hours a week, including warm-up and cool-down, on your strength program.

When many people think of weight training or strength training, they immediately imagine themselves grimacing and straining, looking like the overbuilt heavyweight lifters at the Olympics struggling to raise hundreds of pounds over their heads. Or they envision the oiled hardbodies of the Mr. or Ms. Universe competition. Nothing could be further from what I'm asking you to do.

## Back to Golfing with Gusto

Five years ago, a 72-year-old radiologist came to me because he had developed severe arthritis in both hips and could no longer play golf. Limitation of motion and pain prevented him from using a normal golf swing. He did not want to have hip replacement surgery at this point in time because his pain was not yet severe enough to take that step. He still had pretty good mobility as long as he didn't exert himself or walk for long distances. However, he had retired—and he wanted to play golf.

I explained to him how a golf swing used the strength of his quadricep, back, and abdominal muscles. And I told him that if he would commit to a weight training program for just three months, I believed that he could be back to playing golf on a regular basis—at least nine holes, if not 18.

I set him up with a personal trainer in the local health club associated with my office, and recommended a specific exercise program. His program included

What I'm asking you to add to your health routine is regular, moderate challenging of the major muscle groups in your body. I repeat, moderate. That means lifting moderate weights, ones light enough so that you can lift them eight, 10, or 12 times in succession, according to a reasonable schedule.

With such a moderate program, you can regain a normal amount of strength regardless of your age. But don't limit yourself. Heavy lifting is possible, even for those 70 or 90 years of age. If you start with a program of mild to

some aerobic activity on an exercycle for 30 minutes, five days a week. His strength training program used leg-press, leg-curl, and leg-extension machines and a squat rack. He also learned back strengthening and stretching exercises. And he did 30 to 60 sit-ups every day in any manner that he could.

At the end of six weeks, I saw him back in my office. His mobility was improved and the pain in his hips was reduced by 50 percent. He was taking much less of an anti-inflammatory agent and aspirin for his discomfort. At the end of 12 weeks, he had discontinued the anti-inflammatories and he had begun to go to the driving range and hit golf balls.

At the end of five months, he called to tell me that he had just finished playing nine holes of golf and was now playing every other day.

For the past five years, he has continued his weight training program and has maintained the ability to play golf—without ever undergoing surgery. If a 72-year-old man with severe degenerative arthritis can do this, imagine what people who do not have such limitations could do if they would only incorporate weight training into their exercise programs.

moderate weights, after six months to one year, there's no reason why you can't begin to go for age-group records in weight lifting.

## Three kinds of weight training

There are many types of weight training, but for now I'd like you to consider all of them as falling into one of three categories: calisthenics, free weights, and weight machines.

One of the oldest and easiest forms of exercise—calisthenics—enables you to build your strength by using your muscles to overcome the resistance provided by your own body's weight. Indeed, many people start their weight training by doing nothing more complicated than exercises such as bent-knee sit-ups, front and rear pull-ups, knee bends, leg lunges, and good, old-fashioned push-ups.

The push-up is an ideal example of how calisthenics provide weight training. When doing a push-up, you lift your body right from the floor. In other words, you overcome the physical force of gravity that's pulling you toward the floor. You overcome your body's natural resistance to being lifted. Each time you lift and overcome that resistance, you strengthen major muscles in your arms, chest, shoulders, and back. (There is a modified push-up, done with the knees resting on the floor, for those who initially cannot raise their entire body weight off the floor.)

Let me say now that I think calisthenics are an excellent form of exercise. In fact, I make one calisthenic exercise (bent-knee sit-ups) a continuing part of every exercise program that I recommend. However, there are two drawbacks to calisthenics, and, that's why I don't recommend that you do calisthenics as your only form of body strengthening.

First, if you are older, or if you've allowed your body to really deteriorate, you may find it impossible to do calisthenics—particularly pull-ups and push-ups, where you're required to overcome the substantial weight of your body.

On the other hand, if you are in good enough shape to do calisthenics right away, you will quickly reach the point where the exercises lose much of their effectiveness. You will strengthen your muscles so fast that you will need to do an ever-increasing number of each exercise to derive any benefits, or you will need to add external weights. You can hold a weight plate on your chest while doing sit-ups, or use ankle weights to make a leg raise more difficult than plain calisthenics. But eventually, you reach the point where, in order to get a sufficient workout, you would have to do 100 push-ups with your partner sitting on your back, or 50 pull-ups with a frozen turkey strapped to each ankle.

## Moving to higher resistence

While calisthenics are fine in the beginning, you'll soon want to move on to more sophisticated and efficient forms of exercise. So, I recommend that you start the right way—with a program that involves calisthenics plus some sort of weight or resistance equipment.

There are two basic kinds of strength-training equipment: free weights, including barbells, or long bars with weights at each end, and dumbbells, or bars short enough to be grasped in one hand; and resistance machines. There are many kinds of resistance machines: the standard weight/stack pulley arrangement, rubber cable systems, and shock-absorber systems.

## Making an equipment investment

For the first year you're doing strength training, I recommend that you join a health club instead of purchasing your own equipment. Why?

First of all, it's a great place to make new friends. Secondly, the equipment is usually excellent. Third, you'll be able to get personalized advice from knowledgeable people concerning your exercise program. These people will be able to correct your form, one of the most important elements in effective exercise. They'll also be able to help you adapt your workout to your individual health level.

Finally, most studies reveal that people who buy home equipment use it for approximately 30 to 60 days before it becomes nothing but an expensive hat rack.

Once you've been doing strength training for a year, you might want to invest in your own machine, or just a few free weights for when you can't fit a trip to the gym into your schedule. There are, as you might imagine, positives and negatives associated with any weight equipment you buy.

Free-weight systems offer low cost and convenience. You can set up your gym in almost any room in the house and work out when you wish, wearing whatever you wish. All you need to get started is a barbell with a set of weight plates, at least two dumbbells, and a bench.

Starting weight sets can be purchased inexpensively. Benches vary in price according to their degree of sophistication. At the very least, you want a bench that has a wide, stable base that won't wobble. Make sure it's welded at the joints, not just bolted together—and make sure the padded bench is comfortable. Also check to make sure the uprights (the U-shaped holders that support the barbell off the bench) are wide and strong. You should be able to obtain a complete free-weight set for $200 to $1,000.

Drawbacks to free weights include the need for a "spotter"—someone to help you if you get into trouble using too much weight—and the danger that you might drop a weight on your toe or some other body part during exercise.

Resistance machines offer safety along with the convenience of being able to work out at home (provided you have enough room that you can set aside for a permanent work station). Your best bet for a resistance machine is an all-in-one machine that can be changed into varying configurations to exercise different parts of your body.

The downside to resistance machines is that they're expensive. The typical all-in-one machine retails for about $700, and some cost several times more than that. If you're considering one of these, check to see if there's a reputable used equipment dealer in your town.

My recommendation is that you ultimately work out using one of the resistance machines, but that you start with a combination of free weights and calisthenics. Why? Because it doesn't make a great deal of sense to spend $1,000 or so on a resistance machine until you are positive that you're going to use it. Once you have the "exercise habit," start to look for a resistance machine you like.

I'm not going to recommend a specific machine, because that's a choice you must make personally. Research these machines—their capabilities and their costs—by visiting a local gym and talking to people who use them. Write to manufacturers for literature and visit retailers to comparison shop. Make sure you actually climb aboard any machine you're thinking of purchasing, either in the showroom or at a gym.

## The Value of 'Negative' Work

One of the most important aspects of weight training is overlooked by many trainers. It's the value of what is usually called "negative" work.

When you lift a weight, that action is referred to as the "positive" aspect of lifting. Letting the weight down, or returning the weight to its starting position, is generally referred to as the "negative" aspect of lifting. In the 1970s, Arthur Jones—the founder of Nautilus—recognized the importance of negative work and designed his cam-operated weight machine to make full use of it. He proved that full utilization of negative work in weight lifting actually breaks down more muscle tissue, hence promoting more muscle repair and more build-up of both strength and mass. It not only promotes the building of strength and muscle mass, but also restricts injuries.

To fully utilize the negative aspect, he devised what has come to be called the Nautilus cadence. Exercisers who use this cadence lift weights to a "1–2" count, then pause for a few seconds, and then return the weight to its starting position, slowly and under control, to a "1–2–3–4" count. Though the Nautilus Cadence was originally designed for use by lifters on the Nautilus resistance-type exercise machine, it is now widely used by weight lifters around the world.

Jones provided the ability for individuals to train without injury. That's the bottom line—training without injury. All athletes get injured, but if they could avoid injury, they would be better athletes. If the general population could avoid injury, they would exercise more. Minor injuries are the major reason that people quit exercise, and Jones helped eliminate that excuse.

## Understand a typical workout

Whether you're just starting to do weight training or you're aiming for a retirees' record, there are some features of weight workouts that remain the same.

To get the maximum benefit from your time, you'll want to focus on the major groups of muscles that work together. The groups you should concentrate on are the back muscles, chest muscles, shoulder muscles, abdominal muscles, the biceps (the "front" of your upper arms), the triceps (the "back" of your upper arms), and the leg muscles.

## Warm up first

When you exercise, you stretch not just your muscles but the ligaments and tendons in your body as well. Like a cold rubber band, a tendon or ligament is likely to snap when suddenly stretched. For this reason, it is important that you warm up, slowly stretching and getting your body ready for work, before you actually start to exercise.

The warm-up I recommend is the same regimen I suggest for a pre-aerobic warm-up, namely first stretching, and then slower aerobic exercise. When you stretch, be sure to stretch your arms, legs, and back. An ideal exercise is the "Sun Salutation" that's described in detail in Chapter 9.

Next, gently rev up your heart rate a little bit. Walk on a treadmill or ride an exercycle for five minutes. If you don't have access to either of those machines, jog slowly in a circle for about 15 seconds, then walk for 15 seconds, jog again for 15 seconds, and walk for an additional 15 seconds. Repeat this cycle for about five minutes.

## Setting your weights

In weight training, the object is not to lift as much as you can lift once. The object is to lift what you can comfortably lift a dozen times or so, in order to challenge your muscle groups. Some men and women will find it impossible to lift their own weight, and some won't be able to lift 10 pounds or even five. Others will be able to do pull-ups with ease and raise 100 pounds over their heads without breaking a sweat.

With every exercise, start with a light weight, then increase it in small increments. Experiment. Try an exercise with just two-pound dumbbells—or five pounds or 10. If it's too easy, increase the weight by as little as possible until you find the weight you can lift eight times, but no more.

If you are able to raise a 100-pound barbell over your head one time, you'll find that for exercise purposes, your ideal work-out weight will be about 50 percent of that amount—or about 50 pounds. If you can do one squat with 50 pounds on your shoulders, the amount you can lift eight times will be about 25 pounds.

## Focus on form

Most people who exercise—and most weight trainers—devote altogether too much time and energy focusing solely on the amount of weight being lifted. While there is no denying that the amount of weight you lift plays a major role in determining the results of your exercise, your form, or lifting technique—the position of your body and muscles as you do the exercise—is of major importance, since the proper form insures the best results and helps prevent injuries.

That's why, during the first 12 weeks of your exercise

program, concentrate on form. Make sure you know how to do each exercise properly in order to get the maximum benefits and to avoid injury. Here's where exercising at a health club is beneficial. Usually, either on the machine itself or nearby, are tips on maintaining proper form. And if the exercise doesn't feel right, or you have any questions at all, there's someone there to answer them.

So at first, don't worry about weight levels. Make sure you're doing the exercise properly, and focus on making your training sessions a habit.

## Timing and breathing

Don't rush your workout. Allow yourself about two seconds to lift a weight, and four seconds when you lower it. It helps to actually count those numbers out loud. Make sure you breathe properly. Exhale when you lift the weight or strain against resistance; inhale as you relax or lower the weight. Then, after each set of repetitions, rest for about one minute.

Breathing techniques vary. Though some people do better when breathing in and out through the mouth, I find that one of the best breathing techniques is to use yogic breathing—inhaling and exhaling through the nose. Yogic breathing gives you greater strength with less risk that you'll overexert yourself.

## Rest and repetitions

The time you spend resting between individual sets allows your muscle enzymes to replenish and permits you to lift a weight again and again without damage. In your initial training, rest periods of 30 to 90 seconds will be sufficient.

As you advance in your training, and as the amount of weight you lift in each exercise increases, however, longer rest periods—about 2 or 3 minutes—will allow you to become stronger, build more muscle mass, and prevent the injuries that can occur with heavier weights.

Conventional wisdom has it that sets of 10 to 20 repetitions are ideal to train for muscle endurance, while sets of six to 10 reps should be used to build strength. Lifting any weight more than 20 times or less than six times provides little in the way of benefits, and a lot in terms of injury potential.

## Cool-down and recovery periods

You also need to give yourself a cool-down period. I recommend an easy stretching session and some easy jogging or walking for about five minutes following your weight-training exercise. This will help you to avoid strain and injury.

It's also important to allow recovery time between your exercise sessions. A good rule of thumb is to rest 48 hours between sessions exercising any major muscle group.

In other words, if you exercise your chest and shoulder muscles on Monday, you should wait until Wednesday before exercising that muscle group again. I have found that the most efficient system for the beginner is to work out Monday, Wednesday, and Friday utilizing all muscle groups. The intermediate lifter may choose to exercise four or even five times weekly, but even then should allow major muscle groups to rest and recover between sessions through the use of a "split" routine. With a four-day split routine, the chest, shoulders, and triceps would be exercised two days (Monday and Thursday, for example)—and the legs, back, and biceps would be exercised two of the other days (Tuesday and Friday, for example).

Remember, though, that your lean muscle will be burning calories while you rest, so, even in your recovery period, you are becoming fitter, healthier, leaner, and meaner.

## Bumping up the weights

As soon as an exercise becomes too easy, it's no longer making your muscles stronger. Once you are able to do sets of 10 or 12 repetitions without resting for more than a few seconds between each set, it's time to make the exercise more difficult. You need to work your muscles to the point where they feel almost exhausted after each set of repetitions. If you don't feel that "exhaustion," you're not benefiting from the exercise. At this point, you can gradually increase the weight by a small increment.

As you move from beginner to intermediate weight lifting programs, you can and should seek advice on how to do specific exercises from a personal trainer. Other amateur exercisers will be more than happy to help you out, but their advice may lead you astray and could cause injury. Get help from a professional instead.

## Advanced training techniques

As you move into intermediate weight training, you'll need to know some of the weight-trainer's jargon as you search for ways to safely increase the difficulty of your workout.

You likely already know that each time you lift a given weight in a given exercise is called a repetition, sometimes "rep" for short. A group of repetitions is known as a "set."

And a typical routine might include three sets of 10 repetitions. In other words, you would perform the motion of the exercise 10 times, then rest for a brief period, perform another set of 10 reps, rest again, and then perform another 10-repetition set.

Advanced, trained weight lifters may want to try what's called the pyramid technique. This involves increasing the amount of weight and decreasing the number of reps with each of your three sets on a particular weight. For example, you could lift 100 pounds 12 times in one set, increase the weights to 120 pounds and decrease the number of reps to 10 in the second set, then increase the weight you lift to 140 pounds and decrease the number of reps to eight in the third set. This technique should be used only for a 12-week period of time. Then the program should be changed.

A "super set" is another technique that should be used only by advanced weight lifters. In this technique, opposed or non-related muscle groups are exercised without resting between sets. For example, you might work opposing muscles by doing a biceps exercise and then immediately follow that with an exercise that works the triceps on the same arm, without resting between sets. Or you might perform a chest exercise and then a leg exercise, again without resting. While conventional wisdom maintains that no weight training is aerobic, this type of program does provide aerobic benefit

## Now, let's get down to work!

With the help of a qualified trainer or the staff at your local gym, you should be able to set up a program that safely works all of your major muscle groups.

The major muscle groups, going from large to small,

are legs, chest, back, shoulders, biceps, triceps, and abdomen. The most important group is the legs. The front muscles are the quadriceps which allow you to climb stairs and get out of a chair without assistance. The back muscles are next in importance because they allow you to stay upright and bend and pick up objects without injury. The

## Tips for successful weight training

Here's how to give your workouts the best chance of success.

• Start weight training only if you have already been doing aerobic exercises for at least six months, five days a week, 45 minutes per session.

• Start weight training with an expert's help, in a health club. Don't try to do it on your own.

• Work out regularly. Set a schedule and stick to it as much as possible. The ideal for beginners, again, is three times weekly; you can eventually increase that to as much as five days a week (if you choose). Do this for three months, and I guarantee that you'll be overjoyed with the results.

• Keep a training record. Record how much you're lifting, how many reps you're doing, etc. If you have joined a health club, they will usually provide such charts for you. Your training record will help you decide when to add resistance incrementally. Being able to track your own progress will also keep you interested.

• Drink plenty of water during your workouts.

• Stay with it! Skipping an occasional workout is okay. If you quit for a month or more, however, you'll be right back where you started.

stomach muscles help keep the back muscles from causing injury.

## Don't take weight training lightly

(I intended that pun—honestly I did!) In the beginning of your training program, take it easy. Don't overdo it. Ideally, you can set up a balanced program between free weights and resistance-type equipment. In this way, you'll exercise all of your muscles without any duplication of effort.

Over the decades, I have demonstrated to athletic trainers that I can teach people how to benefit from weight lifting if they maintain their form, rest between sets, and allow muscle groups to recover. The most important aspect of weight training is that you learn it at a pace that allows you to avoid injuries at all costs. I find that personal trainers are sometimes too aggressive. They put everyone into the same mold. Though some people may need to take it a little slower, they will enjoy weight lifting more if they can avoid the soreness and injuries that are often associated with heavy training programs in the beginning.

Remember, most orthopedic injuries occur because of weak muscles and poor flexibility. Exercise safely and stretch regularly, and you'll want to continue exercising for the rest of your life. You'll live to enjoy the many far-reaching benefits of the yang of strength combined with the yin of flexibility.

And remember, just as regular meditation has cumulative effects that go far beyond the benefits derived from just one session, regular exercise will have a cumulative effect on every area of your life. The least you can expect is better health and increased strength at age 70, at age 100, and even beyond.

# CHAPTER 9

# KEEPING YOUR FLEXIBILITY

——— ✦ ———

*What if, when you bought this book, you were in good health and had good habits to begin with? Say, for example, you already exercise aerobically, do strength training, and get good levels of nutrients and antioxidants from supplements and the food you eat. What could possibly go wrong?*

*Injury. Suddenly, your back or knee "goes out," and all your good new habits (or even longstanding ones) go down the drain. Chronic joint or back pain can make it difficult to start or maintain an exercise program. But such problems don't have to be a part of your life. You can do some simple things to banish them forever.*

——— ✦ ———

Flexibility exercises are the essential third component to your exercise program to keep you fit and healthy into your second century. When the masculine, or "yang" influence of strength training is balanced with the feminine, or "yin" of stretching exercises, your risk for pain and injury is reduced.

And let's face it: that potential is high. Back pain is the major debilitating injury in this country. Current figures estimate that up to 85 percent of Americans suffer from lower back pain at least once. Statistics show that back pain accounts for 93 million sick days annually, or about 40 percent of all job absenteeism—a huge cost in terms of lost productivity and profits.

In my experience, the limitations imposed by neck problems run back injuries a close second. Elderly people also often experience stiffness in the shoulders and hips.

Back injuries are the number-one reason athletes retire from playing golf, hockey, tennis, basketball, and baseball. (Shoulder injuries are next, followed by knee injuries in contact sports like football, rugby, and soccer.) The important role that flexibility plays in preventing these injuries is now recognized, and special exercise programs are being introduced in every major sport. The Miami Dolphins football players even use Jazzercise classes as a way to build aerobic balance along with flexibility. Flexibility-focused exercise improves mobility in all the joints of the body.

Everyone wants to avoid such injuries, whether they're a pro athlete or a pro desk jockey. Because in addition to the pain such injuries cause, they diminish quality of life. Joint pain or back pain can keep you from doing the things you want to do. You can't dance, or play, or exercise, or make love, or do much of anything with full enjoyment. Joint or back pain can make strong young men and women whimper like babies.

## Inside your aging back

Chances are excellent that you don't even think about your back until it hurts. That's because it's a remarkable machine that enables you to bend and turn and twist and lift. The primary component of this machine is your spine, which houses your spinal cord and the nerve branches that run off that cord. It also houses about 2,000 muscles and thousands more ligaments. Your spine itself is comprised of 24 vertebrae that are separated by shock absorbers known as discs, plus the sacrum (the bone that attaches your spine to your pelvis), and the coccyx (tailbone).

The spine is, indeed, a remarkable machine, able to function beautifully, until . . . well, until you age.

As you age, the bones in your spine mature. In your mid-20s, degeneration begins. More bone cells are destroyed than your body can replace. At the same time, your spinal discs—those little shock absorbers between the vertebrae—start to lose water content and harden. The muscles in the abdomen and lower back that keep your spine properly erect and curved also begin to weaken, most often as a result of either misuse or disuse. And therein lies the cause of most back pain.

## What causes back pain?

To be sure, some back pain is caused by disease. Hyper-lordosis, or swayback, for example, can cause low back pain, as can cancer, degenerative arthritis, sciatica, osteo-porosis, and other diseases with tongue-twisting Latin names. And scoliosis, a condition typically diagnosed in preadolescent girls whose spines curve abnormally to the side, can lead to extreme back pain if the misalignment is centered in the lower spine, or lumbar region.

In fact, my yoga teacher recently told me that her yoga teacher was born with such severe scoliosis that she was unable to walk a step until she was five years old. Her parents brought her to the yogis and she spent many years of her life learning all aspects of yoga. Today, at age 82, she is vibrant and healthy. She has no physical limitations, and is still actively giving yoga instruction to students all over the world.

However, if you suffer from back pain, it's most likely that your pain is not an indication of scoliosis or osteoporosis, or, in fact, any disease other than a "normal" aching back. Only about 10 percent of all back pain is caused by disease.

## It's strain that causes pain

Your back pain is probably the result of straining the muscles or ligaments in your lower back, either because of an injury or simple overuse. The most common cause of back pain, in fact, is an injury caused by a simple action, like lifting a heavy suitcase the wrong way, twisting suddenly while picking up a package, or bending over too far to retrieve a dropped pencil.

Other common causes of back pain stem from disuse, such as sitting for long stretches in front of a computer, lower back muscle strain during pregnancy, bad posture, or stress.

Since the vast majority of back pain is not caused by an underlying illness, curing that pain is relatively easy. And prevention is as simple as spending a few minutes exercising each day.

## Choosing a flexibility routine

You can choose from many types of flexibility exercises. There are static stretching exercises, martial-arts-based routines, and complete systems of stretches. Two of these, yoga and Pilates, I especially recommend for people who are trying to recover or maintain their flexibility. Chances are, you'll want to combine a complete stretching routine such as the yoga "Sun Salutation" with special stretches for your individual problem areas, or ones that are indicated by what form of aerobic exercise you do.

## Yoga and your life

If I had the ability to somehow force you to take just one action to protect yourself from back pain, I'd command you, starting today, to regularly practice yoga, particularly a single yoga series known as the Sun Salutation.

I myself do this exercise every day, and for the past eight years I have taught it to many of my patients along with yoga breathing techniques. As far as I'm concerned, this is the single most powerful group of yoga poses you can use. It does wonders for all the joints in your body. In addition, it's a great way to deal with stress, to relax, and to achieve mind-body harmony. And it's a great way to warm up before you exercise.

Before you begin any yoga exercise, it's helpful to understand a little bit about the background of this exercise form.

We know for a fact that yoga was in existence at least 2,500 years before the time of Christ, because its practice was recorded in the Vedas, the oldest books in history. It may have been practiced even before that, however, since scholars and archaeologists have unearthed even more ancient figures depicting yogis, or yoga practitioners, in the meditative poses of yoga.

The yogis believe that the body and mind are part of the illusory world of matter, which has a limited life span. The spirit, however, is eternal and passes on to another world when the body wears out. In its purest form, yoga is

## The Right Yoga For You

Some forms of Hatha Yoga are more strenuous than others. So before you sign up for a class, make sure that you can handle it. Ask the instructor what will be involved; tell him or her your age, overall physical condition, and level of familiarity with yoga.

Here are some forms of yoga defined:

• Integral Yoga. This is a gentle class with a fairly set pattern of steady postures, some deep relaxation, and meditation. This type of yoga is ideal for beginners.

• Ashtanga Yoga. Sometimes called "power yoga," this is a vigorous workout with a continuously flowing sequence of poses complemented by deep breathing. It incorporates strength, flexibility, and balance. It should be reserved for people who have had some basic yoga training.

• Iyengar Yoga. This is a precise practice with the focus on correct alignment. The poses are often supported with props (like wood blocks, straps, and blankets). Though slower than the Astanga form, Iyengar is still very vigorous and not for beginners.

• Kundalini Yoga. This form combines breathing techniques, posing, chanting, and meditation—and goes beyond the strictly physical aspects of Hatha yoga.

• Bikram Yoga. This is a vigorous practice that begins and ends with breathing exercises, with a set of 26 poses done in between. The room is heated to at least 80 degrees, and often humidified. This type of yoga should be avoided by anyone who has had recent cardiac problems, high blood pressure, or other vascular problems. However, it is an excellent form of yoga.

designed to enable the union of man's individual spirit with the absolute or pure consciousness. (In fact, the very word yoga means "joining" or "union.")

Practitioners achieve this union by following the three paths of yoga—Hatha Yoga, which focuses on bodily strength and control, Jnana Yoga, which focuses on knowledge, and Raja Yoga, which focuses on mastery of the mind.

Harmony between the body and the mind is achieved by way of assuming postures, or asanas, and practicing breathing that enables you to relax and control your body. People who practice yoga regularly report that, among other things, they become more open to problem solving, more creative, and less stressed by the world around them.

## What yoga can do for you

While yoga is religious in its origins, it need not be practiced like a religion. Millions of people around the world—men and women of all faiths—practice yoga, especially Hatha Yoga, purely for its physical benefits. It is an ideal form of exercise: Anyone can do it—it requires no equipment other than loose, comfortable clothing, and it can be practiced anyplace where there's enough room for you to move without bumping into walls.

Yoga stretches and tones all the muscles and joints, exercising every part of the body. Yoga imparts not only remarkable physical benefits, but emotional and spiritual benefits as well. I believe that it is especially valuable for people in high-stress jobs.

Because yoga involves movement but also regular, controlled breathing, it can serve as an introduction to a physical form of meditation. I find that many people are reluctant to learn meditation. But once they begin to do yoga exercises, the physical benefits make them want to learn more about the breathing and meditative techniques that are often associated with yoga.

I recommend yoga for everyone with high blood pressure, heart disease, cancer, arthritis, and especially for those with back problems. Even though you may begin by using static stretching exercises to treat a back injury, you will eventually need to do yoga (or Pilates) to keep your back healthy.

## The basic Sun Salutation

This Hatha Yoga routine stimulates all 107 of the body's "Marma points"—extremely sensitive pressure points used in Indian massage techniques. I call it my "instant feel-good" routine.

The best time to do the Sun Salutation is in the morning or early evening. Start by repeating the series of poses at least twice; work up to the ability to do six to 10 sets without becoming fatigued or breathing heavily.

Move through the 12 positions of the exercise in one continuous, flowing motion, holding each position, or asana, for five seconds. Your breathing should be continuous and fluid, connecting the 12 movements—except for one brief pause in breathing when you transition between position 6 and position 7. Inhale, expanding your chest, as you extend your spine, and exhale, contracting your abdomen as you bend and flex your spine. If you finish inhaling or exhaling before you are finished holding a position for five seconds, hold your breath until you start to move into the next position. *Be sure to breathe in and out through your nose.*

### THE SALUTATION POSITION

1. Start in the Salutation Position, looking straight ahead and standing straight and tall, with your feet shoulder-width apart and your palms together in front of your chest. (This is also Position 12.)

2. Inhale as you slowly raise your arms up and slightly back in a wide circle, extending your spine and looking up at your hands in the Raised Arm Position. Hold for five seconds. (This is also Position 11.)

### THE RAISED ARM POSITION

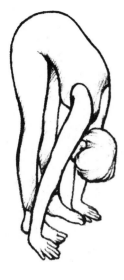

### THE HAND TO FOOT POSITION

3. Exhale as you bend forward as far as you can into the Hand to Foot Position—knees, elbows, and shoulders relaxed, and hands flat on the floor or at your ankles (depending on your degree of flexibility). Hold for five seconds. (This is also Position 10.)

### THE EQUESTRIAN POSITION

4. Inhale as you slowly lunge forward with your right leg, lifting your head and spine as you bend your right knee between your arms and extend your left leg back with the left knee touching the floor in the Equestrian Position. Hold for five seconds. (This is also Position 9.)

## THE MOUNTAIN POSITION

5. Exhale and bring
your left leg forward to
meet your right leg as
you lift your hips and
buttocks into the
Mountain Position,
releasing your spine as
you press down with
your hands, stretch

your heels to the floor (feeling the stretch in the backs of
your legs), and relax your head and neck. Hold for five
seconds. (This is also Position 8.)

6. Without breathing, bend your knees and elbows and
slowly slide your body down, touching your toes, knees,
chest, hands, and chin to the floor in the Eight Limbs Position. Hold briefly.

## THE EIGHT LIMBS POSITION

### THE COBRA POSITION

7. Inhale as you lift your head and chest, pressing down with your hands as you arch your back and bring your shoulders down into the Cobra Position. Hold for five seconds.

8. Exhale as you repeat the Mountain Position, raising your buttocks and hips, and releasing your spine as you press down with your hands. Stretch your heels to the floor (feeling the stretch in the backs of your legs), and relax your head and neck. Hold for five seconds.

9. Inhale as you repeat the Equestrian Position, this time lifting your head and spine as you bring your left leg forward to bend it between your arms, and extending your right leg back with the right knee touching the floor. Hold for five seconds.

10. Exhale as you repeat the Hand to Foot Position, bringing your right leg forward to meet your left leg as you lift your body up and lengthen your spine, keeping your knees, elbows, and shoulders relaxed, and keeping

your hands flat on the floor or at your ankles. Hold for five seconds.

11. Inhale as you repeat the Raised Arm Position, lifting your arms straight up and slightly back as you extend your spine and look up at your hands. Hold for five seconds.

12. Exhale as you return to the Salutation Position, looking straight ahead as you lower your arms and bring your palms together in front of your chest. Hold for five seconds. If you are going to continue with another set, breathe normally in this position for five more seconds before moving into position 2.

13. When you have finished your last set, lie flat on your back for two minutes, arms at your sides and palms up, breathing normally. This is known as the Corpse Position (a resting yoga position). This is my favorite position!

## What yoga can do for your back

I've had patients with 20-year histories of back problems who have reported that regular use of the "Sun Salutation" exercise provided complete backache relief.

There are other yoga routines you can do that will help your back. The two postures below act as a form of mild traction, gently stretching and strengthening the spinal muscles, toning the abdominal organs and stimulating pressure points (marma points) all along the spine. Assume these postures for just a minute or two in the beginning. Then gradually increase the amount of time you devote to each one until you reach the level that gives you the maximum benefit.

## THE DIAMOND, POSITION A

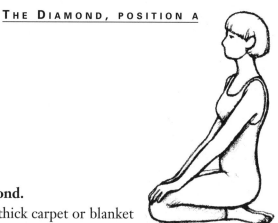

**The Diamond.**

Kneel on a thick carpet or blanket
with your knees close together. Sit
back on your heels with your hands on your knees, and
your back and neck erect. Sit straight so that an imaginary
line passing through your ear, shoulder, elbow, and hip
would be straight (a). Inhale as you slowly lift yourself up
off your heels, aligning your body straight above your
knees (b). Exhale as you return to the starting posture.

This posture can be used to prepare your body for other
postures. It strengthens your
back and your pelvic area.

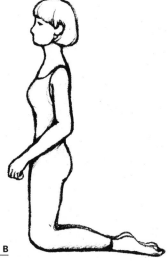

## THE DIAMOND, POSITION B

## THE TWIST, POSITION A

### The Twist.

Sit on the floor with your right leg bent toward your left hip. Bring your left foot across your right leg, placing it on the floor outside it. Bend your left arm across your lower back with the palm of the left hand facing outwards. Straighten your right arm and bring it across your body, grasping your left ankle from outside your left knee as you twist your body to the left (a). Exhale. Turn your head and look over your right shoulder. Hold for a few seconds and then twist to look over your left shoulder (b). (Your shoulders should be at right angles to your body.) Come back to the starting position and repeat on other side.

This is a great posture to alleviate minor lower back pain.

## THE TWIST, POSITION B

## The Pilates method

This system of stretching and strengthening exercises was designed in the 1920s by Joseph Pilates, a dancer, after he was injured. For the last 70 years, dancers in this country and abroad have used Pilates. The same exercise system has recently been popping up in Pilates studios, especially on the East and West Coasts, where both floor and machine-based exercises are taught by instructors who train for a minimum of two years.

Pilates emphasizes challenging the body by its own weight as resistance and by using the abdominal, lower back, upper back, and core muscles to do the exercise movements.

I see several benefits to Pilates. First, it shows you exactly which of your muscles are weak. Second, because it uses your own body weight as resistance, there is very little risk of physical injury. This makes Pilates an ideal choice for anyone with any kind of limitation in any joint. It is even safe for those with back problems.

Pilates stretches and strengthens every muscle, tendon, and ligament. If you look at most professional dancers (or at Pilates instructors) you usually see incredible strength, low body fat, good posture, and a muscular appearance. Something else I've noticed is that they appear to be taller than they actually are. So, if your main goal is to attain the purely aesthetic benefits of stretching, Pilates may be the best program for you.

Although there are some similarities between Pilates and yoga, dance, and the martial arts, a Pilates class can be very strenuous. I have personally experienced 50-minute workouts that left me fatigued, stiff, and drenched in sweat. So I recommend that in the beginning, you should consider one-on-one instruction or go to a very basic class with just a few students so you won't feel frustrated by your own lack of flexibility. Pilates will usually improve your flexibility and strength, but you won't see benefits for two to three months, so don't be discouraged in the beginning.

## Static stretches to prevent back problems

If, like millions of Americans, you suffer from recurring back pain—the kind that never really goes away and flares up from time to time—you'll need to focus on improving the strength and flexibility of particular muscles to free yourself from this kind of pain and injury risk.

These muscles are your hamstrings (the muscles that run down the back of your legs), all your abdominal muscles, and the muscles of your lower back when it's straight and when it's bent. These muscles and ligaments act like the guy that wires that support radio or television antennas, or the lines that support the masts on a sailboat. They allow flexibility with strength.

How do you strengthen those muscles? Exercise, quite simply, must be your number-one backache prevention strategy. This means exercising daily if you already have a back problem, and three times a week if you want to prevent a problem. The muscles of the back and abdomen are the two groups of muscles that it is okay to work daily. We are upright animals and these groups support our posture, so daily exercise, especially flexibility, Pilates, and yoga, is recommended.

Here are a few exercises you can easily do to prevent
back injuries or pain by strengthening your spinal supports:

**Pelvic tilt.**
Lie on your back with your knees bent and your feet flat
on the floor. Using your abdominal muscles, pull in your
stomach while you tilt your hips upward, flattening your
lower back against the floor. Hold this position for 10 seconds and then relax. Repeat 10 times.

THE PELVIC TILT

THE SINGLE KNEE-TO-CHEST STRETCH

**Single knee-to-chest stretch.**
Start in the same position as the exercise above. Pull one
knee into your chest until you feel a comfortable stretch in
your lower back and buttocks. Hold for 10 to 15 seconds.
Repeat with opposite knee. Repeat 2 to 5 times.

## THE BENT-KNEE SIT-UP

**Bent-knee sit-up.**

Lie on the floor with your arms folded across your chest, your knees bent, and your lower back pressed to the floor. Lift your head and shoulders slightly off the floor toward your knees and hold for 10 seconds. Repeat 10 times.

**Sit-and-reach stretch.**

Sit on the floor with your legs stretched and your feet spread apart. Reach forward with your hands toward your feet as far as possible, and slowly return. Do not bounce when trying to reach for your feet. The motion should be smooth.

## THE SIT-AND-REACH STRETCH

### THE ANGRY CAT STRETCH

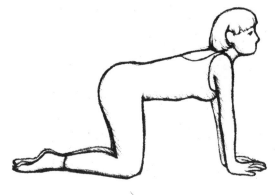

**Angry cat stretch.** Get on your hands and knees with your back level. Slowly arch your back and curl your abdomen, lowering your head and

pulling in your stomach muscles. Hold for 2 seconds and return to starting position. Repeat 5 to 10 times.

**Mid-back stretch.**

Kneel on the floor, extending your arms and torso forward, and sit back on your heels. Reach out as far as you can, keeping your head down. Hold for 10 seconds. Repeat 3 times.

### THE MID-BACK STRETCH

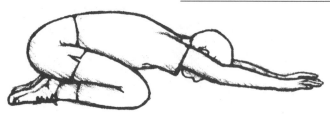

**HAMSTRING STRETCH**

## Hamstring stretch.

Lie on your back with your legs bent. Pull one leg in toward
your chest, supporting the back of your thigh behind your
knee. Attempt to straighten your knee until you feel a comfortable stretch on the back of your thigh. Hold for 10 to 15
seconds. Repeat with opposite leg. Repeat 2 to 5 times.

## Double knee-to-chest stretch.

Lie on your back with your knees bent. Pull both knees
into your chest
until you feel a
comfortable
stretch in your
lower back. Hold
for 10 to 15 sec-
onds. Repeat 2 to
5 times.

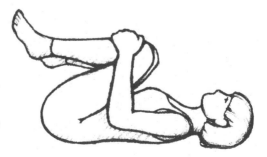

**THE DOUBLE KNEE-TO-CHEST STRETCH**

## You need a total program for the lower back

If you're one of those people who have recurring back pain, the above stretches won't be enough. You will need to learn back strengthening exercises (they may require machines), or do yoga or Pilates in addition to the back exercises. A good program would be back exercises daily and yoga two to four times a week for one hour or a yoga or Pilates class.

You'll need to add exercises to your weight training program that specifically target your lower body. The best exercises for this are squats (knee-bends) and stiff-legged deadlifts. If you have a history of back pain, however, avoid leg curls and leg extensions, since these put stress on your lower back. I would also advise you to avoid standing barbell biceps curls, because if you use too much weight, you'll have a tendency to arch your back for extra lifting power, putting excessive stress on your lower back.

If all of this exercise sounds like a lot of work, remember that has multiple benefits. Sure, yoga exercises will stretch and massage all of your joints and muscles, but you'll also be relieving stress when you start and end each day with the Sun Salutation. While it's true that strengthening your core back and abdominal muscles will take time, those stronger muscles will not only support your back and protect it from injury, but you'll reap all the benefits described in Chapter 8—namely, you'll burn fat faster, your cholesterol will drop, and you'll have better disease resistance.

## Your back-injury emergency kit

If you do have an episode of back pain—and you know

it's because of an injury or strain—what should you do? Here's the course of action I recommend to my patients.

• Some form of manipulation therapy. Even in the case of acute back pain—the kind that comes on suddenly—manipulation therapies are often helpful. As an initial treatment, consider going to a chiropractor, a doctor of osteopathy (D.O.), or an M.D. who does manipulation.

• Rest for a day or two. Avoiding bending, twisting, or lifting as much as possible. Unless it's absolutely necessary, avoid complete bed rest, because it tightens up your muscles. Try instead to lie in a comfortable position, maybe on your side or back with your knees drawn up, perhaps with a pillow between them. This keeps your injury from progressing and allows the swelling of inflamed discs and ligaments to subside.

• Use an ice massage. For the first two days, ice massage usually helps. Take a paper cup, fill it with water, and put it in your freezer. Then have someone rub it in circles on the affected area. Five to ten minutes, three to four times a day is ideal. Ice reduces pain and swelling, and slows the flow of blood to the area to decrease the extent of the injury. However, holding an ice bag or ice pack on your back can cause skin injuries. So if no one is available to give you an ice massage, wrap some ice in a thin towel or a cloth napkin and place it directly on your back for no more than ten minutes at a time.

• After the first 24 to 48 hours, alternate ice with heat. I use a five-minute ice massage followed by moist heat (dry heat does not penetrating to the muscles). If you can lower yourself into a tub of hot water, do so. That's the best way to apply moist heat. If not, use any moist heating pad or an electric heating pad together with a water-soaked sponge-wrap or damp, hot towels. Ideally, use ice massage followed by moist heat four times a day.

• Relieve the pain with bodywork. If possible, use acupuncture, massage, and other forms of body movement such as Trager massage, neuromuscular massage, or body logic to relieve pain. These techniques all help prevent the progression of the injury. If your back pain is extremely limiting, consider electrical stimulation, ultrasound units, and physical therapy.

• Avoid anti-inflammatories if you can. I prefer boswellia, an Ayurvedic herb, or white willow bark, the precursor to aspirin. Take boswellia in a dosage of 500 milligrams two to three times a day; take white willow bark in a dosage of 300 milligrams two to three times a day. I also recommend a homeopathic ointment containing arnica. Homeopathic arnica can also be taken sublingually (under the tongue). If you want to try a pre-blended herbal remedy for back pain, you might also look for these ingredients: burdock, horsetail, and slippery elm. Use the non-steroidal anti-inflammatories (NSAIDs) such as ibuprofen, aspirin, or acetaminophen only as a last resort. And only if you are in truly dire need should you talk to your family physician about prescribing muscle relaxants or prescription strength anti-inflammatories. The former I don't find to be particularly helpful in acute and chronic back problems; the latter can be addictive and can cause unpleasant side effects.

• Call in the troops if necessary. If your recovery requires more than two days of immobility, you may have a more serious problem. Call your doctor for an examination as soon as possible.

• Once you're better, stretch. As soon as your back is less painful, you can start doing the back exercises recommended in this chapter—stretching exercises and the Sun Salutation, and then regular yoga or Pilates classes. Proceed slowly and carefully, but make it happen. It's your best defense against another injury.

## Use common sense to avoid injury

In addition to strengthening your back with exercise, there are precautions you can take to avoid injury or strain in your everyday life.

• Lift smart. If you have to pick up something heavy, don't bend forward from the waist and hips with your legs straight. Instead, bend your knees and rely on your

### When You Need A Doctor

Since some back pain is disease-related, seek medical advice without delay if:

• You suffer from severe back pain that doesn't respond to rest, ice, moist heat, and an anti-inflammatory agent.

• You experience symptoms of weakness or numbness in your hands and feet.

• You have pain from your neck radiating down your arm, or back pain radiating down your leg.

• Your pain—even very minor pain—doesn't improve in a week or so.

• You experience other symptoms, including bladder or bowel problems, along with your back pain.

stronger thigh muscles. Keep your lower back bowed in—not hunched out—when you bend over. Keep the object that you're lifting as close to your body as possible, and never twist or jerk with something heavy in your arms. If you must turn, turn with your feet—not your upper body.

• Avoid static sitting. Don't allow yourself to sit for long periods of time. Get up and take a break. Stretch. Massage your tight muscles.

• If you must sit, sit smart. If your work involves prolonged sitting, make sure that your chair supports your spine—particularly the lumbar area or lower spine. Your chair should also fit your body and support your thighs. Keep your feet flat on the floor with your legs bent at 90 degrees. If your chair doesn't let you do this, you might want to invest in a back pillow and/or a footrest. There are several different types on the market, so you'll have to experiment to find the right one for you.

• Compute carefully. If you do computer work, your screen should be 14 to 16 inches away from your eyes to avoid glare and neck strain. Set your screen at eye level, directly in front of you—not off to the side.

• Get a headset. If you spend a lot of time on the telephone, invest in a headset. Cradling the receiver with your shoulder leads to neck pain.

• Exercise anyway. If you're stuck in a seat for a long time—on a transatlantic flight, for example—you can exercise in your seat. Lift your knee toward the opposite elbow, while reaching the elbow slightly toward the knee. Repeat 15 times with each knee. You can also bend forward slowly in your seat until your chest touches your thighs. Then gently return to an upright position. Repeat about 20 times.

Both of these exercises will stretch the spine and prevent stiffness. They should be repeated every two hours that you spend trapped in your seat.

• Bust your gut. If you have a beer-belly, exercise to get rid of it. Excess weight can push your spine out of alignment.

• If you smoke, quit. Research shows that smoking may reduce blood flow to the vertebrae that protect the disks. So smoking, in addition to all the other problems it can cause, is actually bad for your back as well.

• Reduce stress. Tense muscles are more easily strained. The meditation and relaxation therapies described in Chapter 7 will help make relax your muscles as well as your mind, making stretches easier and helping to reduce your risk of back injury.

## What about sex?

Contrary to what you might think, sex is not harmful when you've got a bad back (provided you don't make love in positions that add injury to injury). It can actually be therapeutic, since sex reduces tension and exercises the lower back.

The trick here is to make sure you're comfortable. Verbalize. Let your partner know exactly what feels good for you and what causes pain.

There are some positions and movements, however, that aren't good for those with weak backs or back injuries.

You'll need to avoid them until your back is healed and strengthened.

Avoid positions that require you to arch your lower back so that your spine is bowed forward, toward your belly. Assuming a "swaybacked" position like this puts a great deal of pressure on the posterior portion of the spine (the back of the spine) and can lead to discomfort.

Don't bend forward with your knees straight—even if you're lying down. Bending forward slightly is okay, provided your knees are slightly bent.

Finally, don't lie flat on your stomach or back with your legs straight. These positions flex the muscles that run from the front of the spine to below the hip joint and put too much forward pressure on the lumbar region of the spine. It's better to lie on your side with your knees slightly bent—or on your back with pillows or other supports under your knees.

Lest you think that following this advice leaves you no choices in lovemaking, here are a few positions that can afford pleasure without aggravating an already painful back.

• Both partners lie on their sides, with the woman's back to the man for rear entry. This is the best position if either (or both) partners are suffering acute back pain.

• If the woman is suffering back pain, she lies on her back with her torso supported by pillows while her lover kneels to support her thighs with his thighs and arms.

• Another good position for a woman with back pain is to kneel astride the man, leaning forward slightly and supporting the weight of her torso on her hands. The same position, with the man's torso raised by a pillow or pillows and his knees bent and supported, is good for a man with back pain. (Avoid vigorously raising the pelvic area, though.)

• A kneeling rear entry position is good for a man suffering back pain, provided that he supports his upper torso on his hands or arms and keeps his back slightly flexed (like a stretching cat). However, this is not a good position for a woman with back pain if she is too active or if her partner puts too much weight on her back.

Pleasurable and therapeutic sex is possible even with back pain. And the extra care and consideration you and your partner show for each other during these times may even pay off with extra dividends as you discover new areas of sensitivity. Experiment and communicate. But don't feel you have to put your sex life on hold.

## Prescription for a pain-free life

The regular practice of the "Sun Salutation," combined with the back-flexibility exercises I gave you in this chapter, plus yoga and Pilates gives you a pretty good "prescription" for maintaining health without injuries—not only for your back but for all areas of your body.

Keep in mind that if you have a back problem, it may take more than six months to regain a strong, healthy, flexible back. It often works to continue to incorporate a multitude of techniques. Some form of realignment (chiropractic, Trager massage, neuromuscular massage, or body logic) on a weekly basis, combined with daily strengthening and stretching exercises, can cure most back problems without the need for drugs or surgical intervention. In addition, the more aerobically fit you are, the less time it will take you to recover from any injury. This is because those who are aerobically fit promote healing by delivering more oxygen and blood to their tissues.

I have no doubt whatsoever that you'll find the effort more than worth it over time. With a strong, flexible back, you'll be able to put in that new garden you've always wanted, go horseback riding with your grandchildren instead of sticking to shuffleboard, or wow your ballroom-dance classmates with a new move. Best of all, you'll be able to do so without the limiting fear of re-injury that is possibly the cruelest part of back and joint pain. You will kiss that fear goodbye, and embrace the new adventures of a strong and healthy future.

# CHAPTER 10

# NUTRITIONAL BALANCE

———— ✦ ————

*Nowhere in the world has nutrition been more carefully analyzed than in the United States. Yet we Americans are notorious for our poor eating habits—and we seem to be getting worse. We are one of the world's most overweight nations. We have high levels of heart disease and cancer. Why? Partly because we don't eat for health. And partly because our recommendations for eating for health have been based on some false assumptions.*

*After years and years of studying nutritional balance and hormones, American scientists are finally beginning to understand some of the chemical reasons for obesity and overweight. And we finally know how you can put these to use to improve your health—both now and into your second century.*

———— ✦ ————

The United States and some other nations are going through a tremendous nutritional revolution, recognizing the many mistakes that we made in dietary recommendations. I am as much at fault as everyone else who taught nutrition for the last 50 years. I used to believe that the number of calories a person consumed could be offset by the amount of his or her activity level.

We now know that this concept is false. You can exercise and exercise and exercise, but if what you eat is unbalanced, you're going to have a difficult time maintaining your ideal body weight. It becomes especially difficult once your body fat exceeds 20 percent for men or 25 percent for women. In other words, if you're overweight, your own body is going to try to see that you stay overweight.

But we also know that chemical hormones that circulate in your blood have a great deal to do with maintaining ideal body weight. Most important, we know that these chemicals can be altered by what you eat. You can make dietary choices to affect your weight.

## My own chubby childhood

I was brought up in an Italian-Irish household, and my mother was a great cook. She commonly served pasta five to seven days a week. While our meals were balanced and we always had vegetables and plenty of fruit, we also had plenty of mashed potatoes, baked potatoes, rice, and the proverbial bread with every meal.

As a result, by the age of 11, I was shopping in the "chubby" section of the boys' clothing department. You can imagine the mental scars this must have created on me and on many other young men my age. By the age of 13, just before I began my career in football, I had developed a serious weight problem. To this day, I struggle to avoid certain foods and to maintain a certain level of activity, because that's what I have to do to maintain my ideal body weight. Fortunately, running and triathlons have taught me how to manage my nutritional program.

In my own medical career, I used to believe that people

should eat a lot of rice, potatoes, pasta, and bread to avoid the complications of a low-fiber diet. However, we have seen that as Americans increased their carbohydrates—from 40 to 50 percent of their total calories to 70 to 80 percent of their calories—they became more and more obese.

No wonder people are so confused about nutritional balance! On the one hand, they are being told that they should be eating more grains, breads, and cereals—and on the other hand, they are watching their health deteriorate.

To show you just one example, the incidence of breast cancer in women in the United States has gone from 1 in 20 women in 1960 to 1 in 8 women in the year 2000.

This deterioration started long before the 1960s. Since 1890, our diets have shifted from being high in complex carbohydrates to high in fat and simple sugars. The typical American now gets about 40 percent to 45 percent of his or her calories from fat, and consumes about 150 pounds of sugar annually.

## Nutritional science—now and then

On a few nutritional issues, scientists' opinions remain unchanged. They still agree that balanced nutrition helps us avoid chronic diseases such as cancer and heart disease. And balanced nutrition helps us maintain our ideal body weight, which allows us to remain physically limber, strong, and full of energy.

But scientific thinking on just what constitutes a balanced diet has changed radically in just the last few years. Despite the fact that the American Heart Association and other organizations have recommended a balanced diet that includes no more than 30 percent fat for the last 15 years, we have continued to get fatter and fatter.

More than 20 years ago, Dr. D. M. Heigsted, professor of nutrition at Harvard School of Public Health in Boston, noted:

> The diet of the American people has become increasingly rich in meat, other sources of saturated fat and sugar. These are the main causes of death and debility in the United States. Ischemic heart disease, cancer, diabetes, and hypertension are the diseases that kill us. They are epidemic in our population.

But today, these diseases are still epidemic. There are more people in the United States with high cholesterol, high triglycerides, too much body fat, low energy, and a sedentary lifestyle than at any other time in our history.

Heart disease, cancer, and stroke are now the top three killers in the U.S. They account for about 75 percent of the approximately 2 million deaths reported each year. These diseases have been irrefutably linked to improper diet. They have been linked to high levels of saturated fat and to a lack of the antioxidants and phytochemicals necessary to ward off changes in the cells that begin the cancer process.

What else does poor diet do to us? It causes obesity, nutritional-variety anemia, gastrointestinal diseases, osteoporosis, and even tooth decay and gum disease.

## Your dietary goal: balance

So what, according to the best, most recent scientific knowledge, constitutes a healthy diet today? How should you be eating to protect your health from these diseases, and preserve it into your second century?

First, you've got to avoid some basic food groups that sabotage health: simple sugars, white flour, and saturated animal fats. Eating a diet that is low in these foods will bullet-proof your body against free-radical damage and the illnesses caused by poor dietary choices. Eating a diet that is high in these foods will expose you to what one physician-researcher called "a free-radical mess."

Second, you've got to eat enough of the right foods: healthy, heart-protecting fats; muscle-building, toxin-free proteins, and phytonutrient-rich fruits and vegetables.

The choices are actually that simple: Eat the right foods in the right amounts, and watch your fat melt and turn into lean, trim muscle with exercise. Stuff yourself indiscriminately at each and every meal, and increase your risk of disease and death. Eat the right foods and extend your life: put the brakes on aging and force it into full retreat. Eat the wrong foods, and watch your body age and decay before your very eyes.

## Eating for health

The primary goals of my nutritional program are health, vitality, longevity, and disease prevention. The way to these goals is to eat a sensible, balanced diet that contains both animal and vegetable protein, is high in fiber, and is loaded with the natural antioxidants that are necessary to prevent disease.

My dietary program will enable you to lose weight if you need to and maintain the ideal percentage of body fat to muscle mass. My program will also help you control your levels of the hormones that lead to aging and diseases of aging—hormones such as human growth hormone, insulin, thyroid hormone, estrogen, and testosterone.

I call it "The Retuning Diet." Because, like a piano, you'll be retuning your body's metabolism to burn stored fat. You'll be retraining your appetite to crave healthy instead of unhealthy foods. And you'll be restoring any of your body's systems that have been damaged by unhealthful eating, helping them work together better to protect you from disease and give you the energy you need to enjoy life.

## Ideal weight versus body-fat percentage

Defining obesity is not always easy. It is complicated by our individual perceptions and by the fact that we tend to accept the idea that gaining weight is simply a natural (and unavoidable) part of the aging process.

As a society, Americans are so used to people being overweight that we often confuse fat with "normal" and healthy. My late friend Dr. George Sheehan, an advocate of running for good health, once said, "If my friends tell me I look good, I know I am too heavy and cannot race or perform as well athletically. If they ask me if I have been sick, and say that I look too thin, I know I am at my ideal weight and will be capable of peak performances."

Unfortunately, our society doesn't tend to see it that way. Patients who come to me with high cholesterol, heart disease, and cancer begin to get down to their ideal weight as soon as I put them on a balanced diet. Their wives often say to me, "Don't you think he's getting too thin?" My response is always the same: "No. Not if his body fat is above 16 percent."

It's a matter of understanding two common terms used in the science of weight loss: ideal weight and body-fat percentage.

## Calculating your ideal weight

Your ideal body weight never changes. You don't get to add ten pounds of fat just because you're over 50, or 60, or 75. So, if you had an athletic body at the age of 18 or 20, that is probably your ideal body weight. Of course, there are some people who were too thin and some people who were too heavy at that age. But the average person was at their ideal weight when they graduated from high school or started college.

I used to tell men that they were probably at their ideal body weight when they finished boot camp. I can't say that any more since so few young men go into the service nowadays. But I bet you've noticed that whenever you see a young soldier in an airport, he is usually lean, muscular—and fitting in that uniform extremely well.

There are, of course, charts you can use to pinpoint the supposedly ideal weight for your age, sex, and build or frame size. These are typically promulgated by insurance companies, and are based on statistical averages. However, there are several problems with these charts.

In the first place, these charts figure in data on individuals who don't exercise (the majority of Americans), pushing the average weights up. Also, the charts reflect changes in the general population over the last several decades. So they have gradually allowed higher weights as men and women in our society have, on average, grown heavier.

And finally, these charts overemphasize the importance of frame size—whether you are "large boned," "average-boned," or "small-boned"—in determining ideal weight. This is, to put it bluntly, bunk. If you and I are the same height, our bones are all the same weight. So the argument that "big bones" excuse obesity is flawed.

In other words, these charts are truly worthwhile only if you want to know the right weight for an overweight, sedentary individual of your age, height, and sex. An individual who is going to be much more prone to the debilitating or fatal diseases of aging than you want to be.

I used to use a formula for men and women that was much better than these standard height-weight charts—but unrealistic for most people. The formula goes like this: Multiply your height in inches by two. Then add 10 if you're a man, or subtract 10 if you're a woman. Using this formula, a 6-foot man would have an ideal weight of 154 pounds (72 inches x 2, plus 10) and a 5'4" woman would have an ideal weight of 118 pounds (64 inches x 2, minus 10). However, I would venture to say that most 6-foot men in the United States who weigh 190 or 200 pounds, and most 5'4" women who weigh 130, think their weight is ideal.

Chances are, your true ideal weight is somewhere between the athletic ideal indicated by the formula and the weight indicated by the insurance company's height-weight charts.

## Calculating your ideal body-fat percentage

Your ideal lean body mass (muscle and bone) also remains the same after the age of 18 or 20. What changes is how much fat you're carrying, and hence, your total body-fat percentage.

For a healthy life at 100, the ideal body fat for a man should be 16 percent or less and the ideal body fat for a woman should be 20 percent or less.

Typically, athletes have more muscle mass and even less fat. So a male bodybuilder's body fat may be as low as 6 to

8 percent, and a female triathlete's may be as low as 10 to 12 percent. However, excessively low body fat in women is extremely detrimental to their hormonal levels and carries health risks of its own. These women often stop having menstrual cycles, and this condition, called amenorrhea, can lead to many problems, the least of which is early loss of bone calcium (osteoporosis) and the worst of which is a higher incidence of certain types of cancer.

In power athletics such as weight lifting and track-and-field, athletes work very hard at increasing muscle mass. They may have a total body weight of 200 or 250 pounds. But as long as their body fat remains below 16 percent (for a man) or 20 percent (for a woman), they will and can live healthfully.

So your body-fat percentage is the most important number for you to know, not your body weight. The "Pinch-an-Inch" test is a simple, very popular, and fairly accurate rule of thumb. If you can pinch an inch or more (especially at the abdomen if you're a man or at the back of your arm if you're a woman), your body-fat percentage is probably too high.

## Get tested by the pros

While you can "guesstimate" whether you're at or above your ideal body-fat level, I strongly recommend that you have this percentage scientifically measured as you begin your new nutritional program.

Getting the accurate numbers will give you a more exact picture of your true physical condition. And if you have your body-fat percentage measured periodically, you'll have a way to measure and celebrate your ongoing progress.

There are three widely used methods for measuring body-fat percentage.

• Underwater weighing. This is the benchmark test, used by athletes for decades. While very accurate, it requires a dunk tank and special scales. It can be a problem for people who are uncomfortable when totally under water.

• Impedance and fiber-optics tests. These measure total body water, and calculate body fat using complex computerized formulas. This test can be troublesome for some men and women because they have to limit their fluid intake prior to testing, and they need to make sure that subsequent tests are all performed at the same time of day to guarantee accuracy.

• Skin-fold testing using calipers. This is the simplest, most common technique. The accuracy of the skin-fold caliper test depends a great deal on the experience of the tester as well as how many folds are measured. I personally prefer this test, because with a little instruction by an expert, you and your partner can test each other.

## How these two figures interact

If you know your weight and you know your percentage of body fat, you can calculate your ideal weight instead of relying on the insurance company charts or your weight when you were 18 or 20.

Let's say I measure 10 percent body fat in a 225-pound male athlete. That means 22.5 pounds of his total body mass is fat. To find out how much of his body mass is currently lean muscle, I subtract 22.5 pounds from 225 pounds and get 202.5 pounds. To find out how much this same individual would weigh at 16 percent body fat—the upper limit of what's healthy—we take that 202.5 pounds, divide it by .84 (100 percent minus 16 percent) and get 241 pounds. It's a big difference, but still within the normal range for a healthy life at 100.

Now, let's say I measure 25 percent body fat—too much—in a 140-pound woman. To calculate her lean body mass, I subtract 35 pounds (25 percent of 140 pounds) from 140 pounds and get 105 pounds. To find out what this same woman would weigh at the healthy maximum of 18 percent body fat, we take that 105 pounds, divide it by .82 (100 percent minus 18 percent) and get an ideal body weight of 128 pounds.

One drawback to this method is that because skin-fold calipers are not accurate enough to give us lean body mass, we have to recalculate ideal weight once the individual begins to lose body fat (when it falls below 25 percent in a man or below 30 percent in a woman). But the same drawback holds true for both impedance and underwater weighing.

## You don't have to do the math

Though it is one of the biomarkers of aging, you don't have to know your exact body-fat percentage to live a long and healthy life. You do, however, have to eat a balanced diet in order to stay healthy and active past your 100th birthday.

And my balanced diet—the post-"Retuning Diet"—is the same for those who want to lose weight and for those who want to stay healthy at 100.

Even if you're out of shape, even if you've put on a few extra pounds, even if your percentage of body fat is excessive and you're suffering from midriff bulge and sagging jowls—you don't have to suffer through a quick-weight-loss diet prior to starting your program of sensible eating unless you are truly obese. Because, if that's the case, your obesity presents an immediate health hazard, and you need to drop 25 or 30 pounds—maybe even more—quickly.

Actually, I think it's a good idea for any man or woman whose body-fat percentage is 30 percent or above to consult with a nutrition counselor or physician practicing nutritional medicine for a sensible weight-reduction program such as the one outlined in this book. Losing weight and keeping it off is not easy, and it is especially difficult if you have already developed any of the health problems that come with being overweight. Seeking individualized medical or nutritional advice can't hurt and may significantly help.

## The theory behind the Retuning Diet

Dr. Barry Sears, one of the people who began to introduce this theory of nutritional and hormonal balance, created an entire program on the premise that your diet should be 40 percent carbohydrate, 40 percent protein, and 30 percent fat.

But this formula is less than ideal because it can be very confusing. However, you can easily achieve a healthy balance of protein, carbohydrates, and fat simply by using the new paradigm of nutrition that I am going to teach you.

According to this new paradigm of nutrition, studies done in the 1930s relating obesity to calories were flawed. (If you don't believe me, simply look at your friends and neighbors and see how restricting fat and calories has affected their weight. The business of selling people "diet" foods has burgeoned—and as a nation, we're more obese than ever.)

## The Metabolism—Body Fat Connection

Some people take in, in a normal day, more calories than they need. They can lose some weight simply by reducing their intake of calories.

On the other hand, once body fat exceeds 25 percent in a man and 30 percent in a woman, the important factor shifts from how many calories you take in to how your body's metabolism manages the calories you do consume. That is why some people can consume fewer calories than they need and remain overweight.

One of the most significant recent advances made in the study of nutrition is the understanding that the body adjusts to changes in caloric intake. This means that if you restrict your calories, your body will readjust its metabolism so you can survive on fewer calories. That's why many people go on an unbalanced diet, lose five or ten pounds, and then their bodies readjust to a lowered caloric intake. Their weight stabilizes; they "plateau," in dieters' lingo. They reduce their calories again, perhaps lose another three or four pounds, and plateau again. They get discouraged, they discontinue calorie restriction, and they gain the weight back.

I call this the "concentration camp syndrome." People who were put in concentration camps during World War II were given minimum nutrients, only water and a small amount of food. While they lost fat and muscle because of starvation, many of them survived for a long period of time because their bodies readjusted to their caloric needs.

That's why calorie restriction diets don't work—and that's why you should avoid them.

This paradigm shift concentrates on nutrition, not dieting or calorie-counting. And my Retuning Diet may conflict with other information that you have read. My program is not like the Dr. Dean Ornish diet, which is laden with complex carbohydrates. It is different from diets that I have favored in the past.

This new paradigm—my Retuning Diet—is based on a simple principle.

White rice, white flour, potatoes, pasta, breads, and simple cereals are the major culprits in dietary imbalances in the United States. And these starchy, nutrient-bereft carbohydrates are unnecessary in your diet.

## Starches equal sugars equal stored body fat

A starch is a simple carbohydrate that is broken down in the body into glucose, or sugar. Especially when eaten by itself, this type of carbohydrate enters the bloodstream, raises blood sugar, and stimulates the pancreas to secrete insulin in order to establish a level of blood sugar that is safe. This blood sugar is then stored either as glycogen or as fat.

But the liver can store only a small percentage of sugar as glycogen, so starchy carbohydrates are stored as fat more often than they are stored as glycogen. We call these starchy carbohydrates "high glycemic index (HGI)" foods.

These foods do more damage than just adding to your fat stores. High intake of HGI carbohydrates incites high blood sugar, or hyperglycemia, which leads to a pancreatic dysfunction. This is no different from the liver dysfunction an alcoholic develops by drinking alcohol. The pancreatic dysfunction causes an overproduction of insulin, or hyperinsulinism. Overproduction of insulin provokes an abnor-

mal retention of fatty acids, thereby increasing the body's
fat reserves. And hyperinsulinism, unaddressed and often
symptomless, can progress into adult-onset diabetes, a disease of aging that puts you at greater risk for the fatal diseases of aging.

## The dangers of hyperinsulinism

I'm going to tell you more about hyperinsulinism, because you may be telling yourself, "Oh, no. That's not me.
I don't have that." Don't be so sure.

The first indicator of hyperinsulinism is an increase in
stored body fat. The second indicator is that the body becomes intolerant to glucose or HGI-laden foods.

Hyperinsulinism—also called pre-diabetes—has a negative effect on your lung capacity because it produces a type
of prostaglandin (cellular hormone) that causes your blood
vessels to constrict. (The good type of prostaglandin causes the blood vessels in the lining of the lungs to dilate.)
Because hyperinsulinism causes a tightening of your blood
vessels, it increases your risk of sudden death from heart
disease, it increases your incidence of asthmatic-type
symptoms or bronchial irritation, and it increases your incidence of high blood pressure.

Hyperinsulinism also lowers your HDL, or "good" cholesterol, which increases your risk of developing high levels of LDL (bad) cholesterol.

The final blow is that hyperinsulinism eventually prevents the insulin from communicating its message to your
cells to store necessary nutrients.

If you are interested in the details of the way all of the
human hormones, including insulin, are interrelated, I
strongly recommend that you read *The Anti-Aging Zone*

by Dr. Barry Sears. However, all you really need to know is that starchy carbohydrates are the most powerful stimuli of insulin production. That's why a diet that is high in carbohydrates and low in protein is so detrimental to your health.

## What the Retuning Diet can do

I originally named the initial phase of my program the "30- to 90-day Retuning Diet." Early on, it seemed that 30 to 90 days was the average amount of time it took for a patient to bring insulin levels down to normal and begin to get down to ideal body weight and fat.

But as I continued to use this program, I realized that it can take six months or more for many individuals to bring their insulin levels down to normal. So now I call this phase of the program simply "The Retuning Diet."

In my practice, I measure my patient's fasting insulin level at a morning appointment. They will have abstained from food for twelve hours, but they should have drunk plenty of water. I then send the patient for a high-glycemic-index meal—pasta or pizza, pancakes, French toast, bread, or cereal—or lots of these foods. Two hours after this meal, and then three hours after, I test insulin levels again. If my patient's baseline insulin is above 20, the two-hour insulin is above 50, and the three-hour insulin is above 40, the patient remains on the retuning phase of my program until insulin levels revert back to normal (20 after a fast and below 30 at one and two hours).

Over the course of the last five years, every single one of my patients who has followed my Retuning Diet to the letter has experienced five things: more energy, a reduction in body fat, a reduction in triglycerides, a reduction in total cholesterol, and an increase in HDL.

If you try my Retuning Diet, I'd like you to keep a diet log for seven days, beginning on your first day. Record what you eat at each meal and between, your weight once or twice during the week, and how you feel. Things to notice include early signs of body fat reduction—your clothes may get loose before your weight shows a change. Your sugar craving should go away in three to ten days and your energy level should rise concomitantly. You may also notice that you are less hungry and that you sleep better. Two months later, do the log again. Then compare this second log to the first one—and prepare to celebrate some dramatic and positive changes.

## Starting the Retuning Diet

So you're embarking on the Retuning Diet. First, I urge you to get your fasting insulin, 2-hour and 3-hour insulin blood levels tested. If you cannot get your insulin levels measured, just follow the first phase of my Retuning Diet for a minimum of 90 days.

After your tested insulin levels return to normal, or after 90 days, you'll continue to eat a balanced diet and keep your HGI carbohydrates to a minimum.

## What you won't eat—and why

I'll give you the hard—not bad, because it's going to be good for your health—news first. Here's what you're going to have to give up to adhere to the Retuning Diet.

**Simple starches.** Absolutely no rice, potatoes, pasta, white flour, or products made from these foods. This

## The Glycemic Index

The glycemic index corresponds to a curve indicating how rapidly your blood sugars rise after you eat specific carbohydrates. Those that cause rapid rising— with an index above 50—are called high glycemic index (HGI) foods.

There's no reason for you to eat most of these HGI foods. Some of them, however are very nutritious. Carrots, beets, and corn, for example, have nutrient-dense properties. And though they should be eliminated from your diet during the initial 30-90 day phase of my nutritional program (more about this a little later), they eventually should be included. But you never need to

| High-glycemic foods | | |
|---|---|---|
| alcohol | 100 | corn |
| refined sugar | 100 | white rice |
| white bread | 95 | beets |
| instant mashed potatoes | 95 | potatoes |
| honey, jam, fruit spreads | 95 | pasta |
| corn flakes and other dry cereals | 85 | sherbet |
| carrots | 85 | bananas |
| candy (brands vary) | 85 | mangoes |
| fruit juices | 85–70 | grapes |
| cookies | 85–70 | |
| condiments | 85–60 | **Low-glycemic foods** |
| (ketchup, mayonnaise, salad dressings) | | meat |
| ice cream | 80 | eggs |

eat potatoes to be healthy. You never need to eat bread or pasta (whole-wheat or otherwise) to be healthy. An elemental diet will get you to ideal body weight and ideal body fat. At ideal body fat, your insulin levels will be normal. And you will have a healthy life at 100.

The numbers in the chart below represent the speed at which sugar/starch molecules are absorbed and put into storage as fat. Beer actually breaks down some tissue to produce fat. The best example is fruit. An apple with 80 calories breaks down slowly; it's used as energy and only 30 percent of the calories are used as fat. On the other hand, a mango with 80 calories is absorbed rapidly and 60 percent of the calories are stored as fat.

| | | |
|---|---|---|
| 70 | cheese | 50 |
| 70 | brown rice | 50 |
| 70 | oatmeal | 50 |
| 70 | fresh white beans | 50 |
| 65 | rye bread | 40 |
| 65 | green peas | 40 |
| 60 | most fresh fruits | 35 |
| 60 | wild rice | 35 |
| 60 | lentils | 30 |
| | chick peas | 30 |
| | dried beans | 30 |
| | soy (any form) | 15 |
| 50 | peanuts | 15 |
| 50 | green vegetables | less than 15 |

includes most cereals as well. Potato chips, cookies, pan-cakes, pastry, and crackers are all on the forbidden list.

**Bread.** Breads are not permitted until after the 30- to 90-day retuning phase of my program—in other words, until your fasting glucose levels are normal (and if you haven't had them tested, you must opt for the 90 days). Eliminate them completely, even whole-wheat bread, rye bread, and heavy grain breads. You will get plenty of fiber from fruits and vegetables. Eliminate sandwiches from your diet and you will automatically become healthier. If you miss a food that you can hold in your hands like a sandwich, try rolling your lunch foods in a big leaf of ro-maine lettuce like a green tortilla.

**Sugar.** No sweetened bread-like foods, no candy, syrups, jams or jellies. Sugar is the arch-enemy of healthy insulin levels.

**Alcohol, caffeine, and artificial sweeteners.** The first purpose of nutrition is to prevent free radicals from stimu-lating cell degeneration. There are certain foods that in-crease free-radical damage. Alcohol is one of the biggest offenders. So is caffeine, and so are artificial sweeteners (with the exception of stevia, a natural herbal sweetener). These three substances also have a mechanism for chang-ing fat metabolism. And they have detriments beyond this.

Caffeine stimulates the heart rate, causes increases in loss of body fluids, and has many other detrimental effects. While there is some evidence to suggest that red wine may have some health benefits, I do not believe that you should be drinking wine on a daily basis. Wine is, after all, fer-mented grapes—and grapes have a high glycemic index (as does alcohol). So during the first 30-90 day phase of my program, you have to eliminate it completely.

The effects of artificial sweeteners on health have never

been studied. However, we know that most people with high body fat who have difficulty losing weight commonly use what we call "diabetic-safe" foods. In my opinion, these artificially sweetened foods cause neurologic problems, loss of mental capacity, and inhibition of fat metabolism.

**Preservatives.** Preservatives added to our food cause free-radical damage that has almost certainly increased the incidence of many diseases, including, most importantly, cancer. We were meant to eat freshly prepared foods. Leftovers and foods that are frozen and put in containers or canned are not as beneficial to your body.

**Most condiments.** Most salad dressings and ketchup contain high amounts of sugar, and mayonnaise contains a lot of fat. Keep away from these bottled non-foods; for a list of other ways to flavor foods, see the "do" list below.

**Certain high-glycemic vegetables and fruits.** These include carrots, beets, corn, bananas, mangoes, and grapes. While these foods are packed with nutrients as well as carbohydrates, they do fall in the category of high-glycemic foods. So you'll need to forego them while you're on the initial phase of the Retuning Diet—in other words, until your fasting glucose levels are normal.

## What you can and should eat

Right about now, you might be saying, "If you tell me to eliminate carbohydrates from my diet, what will I eat?"

Remember, food is medicine. And your body's best defense mechanism against free radicals is to create high antioxidant levels. So you're going to eat foods that are packed with vitamins E, C, selenium, and beta-carotene—some of the important protective antioxidants that help prevent disease from occurring.

Fruits and vegetables will supply you with minerals and vitamins, especially vitamin C; the vegetables will also supply you with beta-carotene and other flavonoids. Oils and nuts will supply your vitamin E; you'll get selenium from cold-water fish. And you'll get omega-3 fatty acids and EPA (eicosapentaenoic acid, which research is proving a very important nutrient for the brain in preventing Alzheimer's disease) from oily fish.

## Here are the building blocks of the retuning diet:

**Protein.** You'll need protein to build and maintain lean muscle mass. You should have approximately 20 grams of protein at breakfast at least three days a week, followed by about 40 at both lunch and dinner. These gram figures are minimums, so there's no limit on the size of your protein portions. You should, however, avoid the protein sources that are high in saturated fat, such as bacon, sausage, and t-bone steaks. Avoid processed meats—such as hot dogs and cold cuts—because they're high in both saturated fats and preservatives. Go for leaner cuts, grill or broil when possible, and buy organic (or at least hormone- and antibiotic-free) meats when possible.

While fish is a great protein source that provides beneficial oils as well, avoid the "bottom feeder" types of fish. They are scavengers, and the things they eat are the most likely to have died from unnatural causes. Such seafood includes all shellfish, grouper, and flounder. Surface fish such as tuna, mackerel, mahi mahi, salmon, and trout are all excellent.

(A note for fish-lovers: Many of our major bodies of water have been contaminated with mercury. If you consume large quantities of fish—five or more servings a week—or you do not know if the fish you eat are farmed or which body of water they come from, I strongly suggest that you take at least one gram of whole-food chlorella daily. Take an additional gram every time you eat fish or take fish oil capsules. Chlorella is a one-celled algae that is an excellent detoxifier of mercury and other heavy metals.)

**Vegetables.** Eat at least one cooked vegetable at lunch, and two cooked vegetables at dinner. During the retuning phase, your body is still in a hyperinsulin state. One of the things this means is that your body doesn't digest raw foods well. So you can eat salads, but they won't give you the nutritional benefits that cooked vegetables do. So they can't be your main meal, and they don't count as one of the three cooked vegetables that you must eat each day. If, for example, you have a choice of either a chicken caesar salad or a cooked chicken breast with spinach, broccoli, and a side salad, choose the cooked chicken breast with spinach, broccoli, and a side salad. The good news: your vegetable portions can be unlimited in size.

**Fruit.** Despite the fact that there are some high-glycemic fruits (mangoes, bananas, and grapes), most fruits have a low glycemic index. However, when combined with other carbohydrates or proteins or fats, fruits tend to be digested more slowly, ferment in your gastrointestinal tract, and be absorbed as simple sugars. That's why fruits are best if eaten alone as a between-meal snack—either at least 20 minutes before a meal, or 1 1/2 to 2 hours afterward. Never eat fruit after 7 p.m. While some diets eliminate fruit completely, I feel that fruit is so powerful as an antioxidant that you should eat at least two servings of fruit every single day. However, this doesn't mean fruit juice. Juice gives your body too high a sugar load.

**Yogurt.** Plain, fresh yogurt is an excellent food because it has a perfect balance of protein, carbohydrates, and fat. However, boxed, flavored yogurts are usually too high in carbohydrates. Look at a carton of vanilla yogurt. (Vanilla has no calories, it is simply a flavoring added to make the yogurt taste good.) Then look at a carton of plain yogurt and compare the two carbohydrate levels. The vanilla yogurt probably has higher carbohydrate levels because it contains added sugar disguised as fructose or maltose or corn syrup. This means that all fruited yogurts and sweetened yogurts (whether the sweetener is sugar or aspartame) are out. In my opinion, frozen yogurt falls into the category of non-foods. It usually has so many additives to give it color, consistency, and a sweet taste that it has no benefits at all.

**Cheese.** Cheeses, especially low-fat cheeses and some hard cheeses, are permitted on my program because they are not HGI foods. However, they are often high in saturated fat and therefore should be used in moderation. Feta cheese, part-skim-milk mozzarella, and other types of low-fat cheeses are permitted. Goat cheeses are good because they are low in saturated fat and sugar. Yogurt cheeses are okay, as are soy cheeses, so long as they are unflavored. Nonfat cheeses contain too many preservatives; don't eat them.

**Cereals.** Dry cereals that contain less than 2 grams of sugar are permitted on my program. These are healthy foods. But, as you'll notice as you read the labels, most cereals are extremely high in simple sugars. If you want to eat cereal for your morning meal, cream of wheat, shredded wheat, Fiber-One, and Kashi are all excellent choices.

**Fats.** Fats are essential to your diet because they contain certain vitamins (E, D, K, and A) and the omega-3 and omega-6 fatty acids that are necessary to produce good prostaglandins in your cells. All fish oils (like tuna, mackerel, and salmon) are rich in essential fats and permitted on my program. Unsaturated fats like olive oil, grapeseed oil, safflower oil, canola oil, and ghee (clarified butter) are also permitted.

Butter, which has saturated fats, is permitted in limited amounts, between one and two tablespoons a day. However, hydrogenated fats like margarine are high in trans-fatty acids and should be eliminated from your diet forever. Solid fats like lard are very high in saturated fat and should be eliminated. Liquid fats are low in saturated fat, and all the nut oils, including peanut, sesame, almond, and walnut, are okay to use. You can use fats to flavor food but don't overdo them because many foods, such as fish and beans, contain natural fats.

**Fiber.** Fiber is an important nutrient. Foods high in fiber help prevent the onset of many illnesses and keep your gastrointestinal tract healthy. Good sources of fiber include dried beans, lentils, chick peas, fresh fruits, cabbage, mushrooms, asparagus, okra, spinach, and all cooked vegetables. Yes, you can get fiber from bran and whole-fiber cereals and brown rice. But refined flours are low in fiber. And dried fruits, though high in fiber, have a high glycemic index and are therefore not on this diet

If you experience constipation on the Retuning Diet, there are four steps to take. First, increase your water intake. Second, remove dairy from your diet. Third, add bran or psyllium husk powder to your diet. Finally, you can use prunes, stop eating salad, and consume only steamed and stir-fried vegetables until the constipation stops. You may also use herbal supplements at night to soften stools.

**Water.** Drink at least 8 to 10 glasses of water per day. Room temperature or hot water is preferable to iced water.

Ice-cold water slows down your digestion.

Also, drink as little as possible with your meals. Water drunk with meals dilutes your digestive enzymes and inhibits the absorption of nutrients.

**Other beverages.** All herbal teas are all permitted on my program in unlimited amounts. So is green tea. (Even though green tea has caffeine in it, it does minimal damage because it has such high antioxidant levels.) However, limit yourself to decaffeinated coffee or tea—and no more than two cups a day of each.

## Other Retuning Diet details

Here's what your eating routine will look like with the Retuning Diet.

**Breakfast.** You'll start your day with fruit—grapefruit, melon, berries, pears, apples, or peaches. Twenty minutes later, have some hot oatmeal with almonds. Or shredded wheat with skim milk. Or you might make yourself an omelet using four egg whites and one whole egg, plus spinach and feta cheese. For your beverage, choose either hot water and lemon, herbal tea, or decaffeinated coffee.

**Mid-morning snack.** Fruit. (But remember to avoid bananas, grapes, and mangoes during the retuning phase.)

**Lunch.** At least six ounces of protein from animal or vegetable sources. So fish, chicken, a vegetable burger, tofu, tahini, lentil or split pea soup, or vegetable soup. (But remember to make sure there's no rice, potatoes, pasta, corn, or carrots in the soup. And don't add crackers.) At least one cooked vegetable. Salad with balsamic vinegar, olive oil, canola oil, or a little peanut oil. You can add nuts and seeds or some feta cheese or a small amount of mozzarella to the salad. Also any raw vegetable that is not a

HGI—broccoli, tomatoes, cucumbers, onions are okay; carrots are not. And no bread and no croutons.

**Afternoon snack.** Fruit.

**Dinner.** At least six ounces of protein. Two cooked vegetables of different colors—for example, summer squash and okra, or asparagus and cauliflower. Or you can have these vegetables in soup. A large salad, similar to the one you had at lunch.

**Evening snack.** I hesitate to include this because ideally, you should not be snacking late in the evening. It reduces your brain's production of melatonin, which is necessary for deep and restful sleep. It inhibits production of growth hormone, one of your body's major anti-aging chemicals.

If you must snack at night, make sure you eat nothing for at least two hours before you go to sleep, and that you eat no fruit after 7:00 p.m. Plain yogurt is a good snack, and although I don't recommend consuming a lot of dairy products, skim milk is okay. A better choice would be something balanced like a small can of sardines, or a little tuna with salad, or a small portion of chicken breast with spinach.

## Beyond the Retuning Diet

Once you get your insulin levels below baseline, you can go on to the next phase of my program.

The second phase of my nutrition program allows you to have some amounts of some foods that were completely eliminated from your diet during the retuning phase—carrots, beets, corn, bananas, grapes, and mangoes for starters.

You can also add some starchy foods back into your

diet, but you'll need to eat them in moderation so that your insulin levels remain stable. Restrict potatoes to no more than 1 or 2 per week, and choose sweet potatoes in preference to white, boiled potatoes in preference to mashed. Eliminate white rice from your diet forever, except basmati, a whole-grain white rice. Eat it or brown rice no more than three times per week. You can also use millet, barley, and quinoa. If you must eat pasta, make sure it is made from whole grains, and try to eat pasta as a side dish, not as a meal. Or combine it with an ample amount of protein. Make sure the breads you eat are rye or whole-grain; ideally, eat them only at breakfast.

Drink no more than two or three glasses of wine per week, or one drink of distilled liquor per week. And never drink beer. It promotes fat production. The consumption of any alcohol produces a craving for sugar so it's best to stay away from it.

Ideally, you should eat three meals a day. But they don't have to be huge meals in the typical American style. I recommend that you follow the lead of other cultures that have maintained good health and sound nutrition. Eat a light breakfast. Then eat your main meal of the day before 2:00 p.m. Finish with a light evening meal, and if possible, don't eat anything after 7:00 p.m.

You don't have to wait until you achieve your ideal body fat percentage in order to move on to the second phase of my program, as long as your fasting insulin levels and your two- and three-hour insulin levels are normal. If you are not able to measure these levels, stay on the Retuning Diet for a minimum of 90 days, or at least until you have lost approximately 8 to 10 pounds of body weight.

## Why You Don't Need to Count Calories

You can live as long as seven months with water alone and no food. However, during that time, your body will begin to break down your protein-fat stores. Changes will also occur in your liver and other organs. As long as you have fluids (water), the organs themselves can be used as nutrients, and you can survive. That's why it's not a good idea to restrict your calories below 1,000 if you're a woman or below 1,200-1,500 if you're a man. And that's why I no longer believe that calorie counting has any value in nutritional programs.

Like many others who have studied nutrition, I believe that food is fuel and that if your body has a balance of the right fuel, you will use your stored body fat as energy—without restricting calories. That doesn't mean you can eat anything that you want to eat. But if your diet is a balance of essential fats and protein and carbohydrates from fruits and vegetables instead of carbohydrates from simple sugars, you will eventually get to your ideal body-fat percentage.

Here's the only thing you need to know about calories.

A calorie is a heat unit that is used by nutritionists. One thing that always confuses people is that one gram of carbohydrates or protein provides fewer calories than one gram of fat. On average, while there are variations from one food to another and from one person to another, every gram of carbohydrate and protein produces four calories. Every gram of fat produces nine calories. While calorie counting is of no value to you now, it is important to know that if your diet is too high in fat, it is just as unbalanced as if it is too high in starchy carbohydrates or protein.

## Keeping your diet healthy for life

Once you've reached your ideal weight and body-fat percentage, I hope that you won't want to return to your original poor eating habits. I hope you'll feel so much better and have so much more energy, you'll want to adapt your eating habits to ones that will keep you vibrant and disease-free into your second century. But if you do find yourself sliding back into old habits, you can just go back on the Retuning Diet. Or you can keep the following general principles in mind.

Eat plenty of cooked vegetables and fruit on a regular

### Buying and Eating the Best

Our nation's soil has changed over time. It has been depleted of the nitrogen necessary for balanced trace-mineral intake, and has been contaminated with chemicals. We can no longer depend on food to provide us with all the vitamins we need. Beta-carotene levels in carrots, for example, vary from bunch to bunch, depending upon where the carrots were grown. For this reason, too, I recommend organically grown products, purchased as fresh from harvest as possible. If you can buy your fruits and vegetables from an organic grower at a local farmer's market, that's often the best way.

By the same token, you should seek the highest quality in any animal foods you eat. That means buying organic or at least hormone- and antibiotic-free eggs, meat, and milk where possible. It sometimes costs more, but there are ways to trim that extra cost by buying in bulk or joining buying groups and purchasing directly from the producer.

basis. Always look at the variety of foods and colors on your plate. Generally speaking, the more colors on your plate, the more balanced your diet.

Essential fatty acids are important. These compounds help your body produce the right kinds of prostaglandins. So make sure that your diet includes almonds, walnuts, seeds, some safflower and canola oil, and grapeseed oil on a regular basis. Just substitute these healthy foods for some of the unhealthy staples of a typical diet—such as chips, French fries, and ketchup.

Fish are an excellent source of omega-3 fatty acids. If you don't eat fish, you can still get your omega-3 and omega-6 fatty acids from flaxseeds or flaxseed oil.

Vitamins, minerals, and fiber are crucial. In fact, you should get 30 grams of fiber a day. You'll get this much if you're eating 3 or 4 cooked vegetables a day, and unlimited amounts of green leafy salads combined with raw vegetables. You should also take advantage of vegetable sources of protein such as soy protein, soy beans, mung beans, bean sprouts, lentils, and chick peas.

Continue to limit HGI carbohydrates as much as you can. These foods aren't so bad for you if you eat them once in a while. But you can usually choose something that gives your body more nutrients and fewer sugars—and often something that tastes just as good and is just as satisfying. As you continue to eat a mostly balanced diet, you may find that you don't enjoy these high-carbohydrate foods. You may even find that you don't feel well after eating them.

## It's about making intelligent choices

The most important thing about changing your diet is

that it will be your choice. You can change your eating habits—a little bit or a lot. You can make some appropriate choices today and wait six months or a year or two years and then make more choices.

I have learned that when it comes to making changes, it is best to make small changes that you stick to rather than trying to change your diet and exercise patterns, and begin meditating and doing yoga and weight training—all at the same time. Making dietary changes, like all the other changes I'm recommending in this book, is something you can and should continue to re-evaluate throughout your life.

## Exercise and Weight Loss

You could do it without exercise—but why would you want to?

It's not essential to exercise in order to lose weight. However, I cannot imagine a person with an ideal body weight or ideal body-fat percentage who doesn't exercise.

The main purpose of exercise is not weight loss, it's overall health improvement. Remember that oxygen is the fuel of the body, and the heart pumps oxygen to all your organs. The more oxygen your heart can pump, the more efficiently your organs perform. And exercise strengthens your heart.

Exercise improves eyesight, sexual performance, kidney function, liver function—and most importantly, it preserves your cardiovascular system so you can stay healthy into your second century. It builds stronger, healthier bones. That's why osteoporosis does not become a problem for people who exercise regularly. And people who exercise every day have an easier time

You can, if you wish, become a dietary reactionary, eating little more than nuts and berries, and cutting out all meats and dairy products (many individuals I know and respect have done so). You can drink alcohol in moderation, or swear off it forever. You can have ice cream for dessert, or not. You can drink a couple of cups of coffee each day, or forego caffeine completely. The choices are yours.

The important thing is that you make informed choices. That you stop blindly putting food and drink in your belly without paying attention to that food's impact on your health.

maintaining correct body-fat ratios.

Exercise is not as critical for weight loss as I used to think it was. But it's still as important to overall health— and it does make weight loss easier. To maintain health and lose weight, I recommend 45 minutes of aerobic activity five days a week. I realize, however—and I want you to realize—that you can achieve ideal body fat without doing aerobics if you eat a balanced diet, go to the gym, and lift weights every day. Weight lifters always maintain ideal body fat. Part of the reason is that they know how to eat a balanced diet.

While exercise does help maintain ideal body fat, it also shifts the way your metabolic system works. Exercise improves the function of the thyroid gland because it increases oxygenation. Exercise allows muscle mass to be maintained while fat stores are used as energy. Exercise is the medicine of the future.

Ask me if you can achieve ideal body weight without exercise, and I'll say, "Yes, you can achieve ideal body weight. But you cannot achieve ideal body health."

## Bad Diets, Fad Diets, and Yo-Yo Diets

A quick word here about fad diets (I define this as any diet that has a name, like the "Pound-Buster Diet" or the "Hot Fudge Diet"). Fad diets don't work! Though many of the fad diets you read about or see advertised on television may work in the short run, they don't work long term. They don't achieve permanent non-obesity.

Fad diets—on which Americans spend billions of dollars every year, seduced by the promise that they'll lose huge amounts of weight in 10 days or two weeks—are not truly diets. They're programs of either planned semi-starvation or unbalanced meals that strip your body of important nutrients. They may strip weight away by eliminating some of your fat reserves, but they also waste lean muscle.

But muscle mass is important if you want to stay healthy and age gracefully. Unbalanced high-carbohydrate, high-protein diets also deplete the body's stores of amino acids, and they can leave the elderly in a weakened state. When they are discontinued, the weight almost always comes back—but instead of returning as the muscle that you've lost, it returns as fat.

Let's assume you weigh 200 pounds and have 30 percent body fat. That means 60 pounds of your total body weight is fat. If you go on a fad diet and lose 20 pounds, not all of that weight will be a loss of your fat reserves. At least part of your weight loss—probably one-third of it—will come from muscle.

If, like most dieters, you don't follow up that quick weight loss with a sensible diet, you'll quickly gain back the 20 pounds you lost. But—and this is an important "but"— you will regain the weight as fat, pushing your body weight to 33.3 percent fat. You now have 66.6 pounds of fat instead of the 60 pounds of fat you started with.

When you become a "yo-yo" dieter, you lose muscle and gain fat every time your weight goes up and down. This is a notorious problem for women going through menopause, when their estrogen-progesterone levels and thyroid hormone levels fluctuate.

Diets that are high in protein and low in carbohydrates— or have no carbohydrates—are also unhealthy. They can drive your insulin levels too low, causing low blood pressure, fatigue, irritability, increased hunger, and even loss of muscle mass. Then, as soon as you go back to a normal, balanced diet, your body fat stores shoot up. So avoid these types of diets altogether.

And don't waste your money on allegedly "low-fat" foods. These products may still derive as much as 80 percent of their calories from fat, because they include the water weight in their products in their calculations. Artificially sweetened and nonfat foods are just not nutritionally good foods. That's why I call them "non-foods."

## Do it your way

Experience teaches me that when you start eating a healthy diet, you'll be so satisfied that you won't want unhealthy foods. It also teaches me that once you start to eat properly, you'll realize how great you feel, and you'll want to make even more changes over time.

In my own case, for example, I first tried a vegetarian diet for one month—as a joke—way back in 1977. After that month was up, I realized I felt wonderful, and I haven't had a piece of red meat since that day.

By improving your diet and nutrition, in your own way and at your own speed, you will make a positive step toward determining not just how long you'll live, but also how well you'll age.

## Menus

The menus on the next pages represent meals that persons who have completed the Retuning Diet should eat. If you are still on the Retuning Diet, you may adapt the menus using these rules: First, do not eat rice (not even brown rice), bread (not even whole wheat), or pasta. And second, do not combine fruit with your meals. Eat the fruit that's in these menus only twenty minutes before a meal or ninety minutes after a meal.

## Vegetarian Dine-Out Menu

### Breakfast
1 cup oatmeal with cinnamon
2/3 cup soy milk or 2-percent milk
1 tablespoon chopped English walnuts
1 link soy sausage
1 cup seasonal berries
1 cup herbal tea

### Lunch
1 cup minestrone soup
eggplant parmesan with marinara sauce and
    mozzarella
steamed spinach with olive oil and lemon
    (ask server for a sprinkle of pine nuts)
1 green salad with balsamic vinaigrette
1/4 cantaloupe

### Dinner
miso soup with seaweed and scallions
veggie stir-fry with seitan or tofu
brown rice
salad with miso/shiitake mushroom dressing
gingered fruit

### Snacks
1 Valencia orange with 1/4 cup walnuts
or
1 cup strawberries with roasted almonds

## Vegetarian Dine-In Menu

### Breakfast

berry smoothie, made with whey Protein powder,
 6 ounces soy milk, 2/3 cup seasonal berries
1 tablespoon unsweetened, natural peanut butter
vegetable patty or soy sausage link
1 cup green tea

### Snack

sliced papaya with lemon

### Lunch

lentil soup with soy sausage links
grilled peppers, eggplant, zucchini, and squash drizzled
 with extra virgin olive oil

## Look to the East for Wise Eating

Many Eastern countries have food philosophies that help guide them to healthy food choices. The Japanese, for example, reject our four food groups and choose foods for their yin or yang qualities. Yang foods, for example, are used to bring yin people (those with high mental activity) into balance, and yin foods are used to bring yang people (those who are more physically active) into balance.

Ayurvedic practitioners believe that food constitutes the most important path to health. They divide food into six tastes: sweet, sour, salty, astringent, pungent, and bitter. Like the Japanese, Ayurvedic practitioners use food to balance the physiology of the human mind-body. Foods that are sweet, sour, and salty are used to pacify the mentally active "vata" types. Sweet, bitter, and astringent foods are used to calm the fiery "pitta" types. And, finally, the pungent, astringent, and bitter

1/2 cup hummus, over Greek salad made with organic
greens, tomatoes, cucumbers, feta cheese and
Kalamata olives, 3 ounces grilled tofu, olive oil
and lemon dressing

**Snack**

strawberries

**Dinner**

vegetarian chili made with ground soy burger patties,
kidney, black, and navy beans
steamed kelp with lemon and olive oil, sprinkled with
almonds
grilled butternut squash
green salad with miso dressing

foods are used to activate the somewhat lethargic "kapha"
types. Ayurvedic principles instruct that each meal should
incorporate all six tastes to some degree. Another
Ayurvedic principle teaches us that meals should be prepared with love, and eaten in a calm, peaceful environment.

Outside of America, food is almost always understood for
its medicinal value. Ginger is used in India and China as a
digestive aid, and also to relieve nausea, indigestion, heart-
burn, and the vertigo of motion sickness. Garlic controls in-
fections, colds, flu, hypertension, and cancer. Fenugreek is
used in Chinese tea as an aphrodisiac and as a breast cancer preventive.

I could go on for pages and pages with more examples of
the way food is used in other cultures to create health
rather than to cause disease. If we as a nation are going to
reduce our obesity and our high incidence of diseases, we
must learn that moderation and balance are the keys to
healthy nutrition.

## Semi-Vegetarian Dine-Out Menu

### Breakfast
1/2 grapefruit 20 minutes before breakfast
Mediterranean omelet made with tomatoes, spinach,
    and feta cheese
decaffeinated beverage

### Lunch
1 cup green salad with miso dressing
1 cup stir-fried veggies with ginger/tamari sauce
5-8 ounces grilled salmon with teriyaki sauce
1/4 cup brown rice

### Snack
Orange and apple slices with ginger

### Dinner
tomato-basil-mozzarella salad with olive oil and
    balsamic vinaigrette
5- to 8-ounce grilled tuna steak
1/2 cup baked acorn squash
wilted spinach with extra-virgin olive oil
1 cup steamed cauliflower topped with 1 tablespoon
    walnuts, sprinkled olive oil, and lemon juice
cantaloupe

## Semi-Vegetarian Dine-In Menu

### Breakfast
cantaloupe chunks 20 minutes before breakfast
rolled oats with part-skim milk sprinkled with
    cinnamon and walnuts
soy sausage or smoked salmon
hot decaffeinated beverage

## Lunch

1 cup split pea soup

shrimp marinara over spaghetti squash

spinach patties with sun-dried tomatoes

tomato-caper-arugula salad with balsamic vinaigrette

## Snack

poached pears

## Dinner

cucumber salad with olive oil, lemon and 2 Kalamata olives

Mediterranean snapper with tomato-caper-lemon sauté
sauce

Grilled eggplant and fennel

1/3 cup lentils or 1/3 cup brown rice

apples with cinnamon

## Snacks

1/4 honeydew

or

1/2 cup lowfat plain yogurt with 1/4 cup berries

# Meat-Eater's Dine-Out Menu

## Breakfast

cup of fresh fruit chunks 20 minutes before breakfast

Western omelet made with green pepper, onion,
cheddar cheese, onions, and turkey bacon

herbal tea

## Lunch

minestrone soup

London broil

string beans with sesame seeds

garden salad made with romaine lettuce, shredded carrots,
tomatoes, and cucumber with cilantro vinaigrette

### Snack

poached pears or other fruit

### Dinner

chicken Florentine

caponata

spinach salad with walnut oil dressing

fruit gelatin with nuts

## Meat-Eater's Dine-In Menu

### Breakfast

orange slices 20 minutes before breakfast

2 poached eggs over whole grain toast

1-ounce low-sodium Canadian bacon

tomato slices

Decaffeinated beverage

### Lunch

1 cup black bean soup with scallions

4-ounce lean burger patty

grilled zucchini, summer squash, and red bell peppers

romaine salad with raw veggies, olive oil, and vinegar

### Snack

strawberries with balsamic vinegar

### Dinner

chicken escarole soup

veal piccata

roasted eggplant with olive tapenade

spinach patties

green salad with balsamic vinaigrette

blueberries

# EPILOGUE

*A mind that is fast is sick.*
*A mind that is slow is sound.*
*A mind that is still is divine.*

— *Meber Baba*

As I completed this book, I realized that there were many lessons that I had not taught. *AGEproofing* clearly deals with the physical body and how to improve it. It also discusses how to use the mind to improve health. My greatest realization was that *AGEproofing* is the very beginning of the journey to perfect health.

When I was training for athletic events such as a marathon or the IRONMAN triathlon, I used to say, "The race is not as important as the training to get to the race." You see, the race is just an event, while the training is the journey to being fit enough to compete in the race. This is the truth that I want readers to see: *AGEproofing* is a journey, not an event.

Changing your lifestyle takes time; that is the journey. Changing your body physically is an event. Eating the right foods, taking the correct supplements is another event. The purpose of the journey is to achieve good health and longevity.

Mental attitude, happiness, and your emotions are also part of the journey, but they are just events in the journey. Mind exercises, relaxation therapy, and meditation and prayer—all of the things you do to achieve good health— are events that occur during your journey.

But the journey to the stillness of the mind ends in the spiritual realm, the path I have yet to teach you. All of the aspects of the spiritual realms of health and healing are the next step in the journey. The purpose of this epilogue is to let you know that your journey to health is a continuous series of events that lead to balance in the mind, body, and the spirit. When you are out of balance, then and only then does illness present itself.

As you were reading *AGEproofing* you should have experienced a sense of control over your own destiny—that is, the knowledge that the choices you make determine the length of your physical life. You are truly in control of your health. Bad choices lead to bad outcomes. Good choices lead to productive longevity.

Do not fool yourself into thinking that you can drink alcohol, smoke cigarettes, and eat high-sugar foods and live to 100 years. It may happen by accident, but not by design.

## The physical realm

Consider this: First, you have to know what health risks you have. Heredity and the lifestyle choices you make determine the health risks. Once you are armed with knowing what illnesses you are most likely to develop, use the steps in *AGEproofing* to begin your journey. Remember, it is not necessary to change everything at once; take one step at a time if you choose.

I may prefer for you to start with nutrition, by eating the right foods. You may want to embark on an exercise regime. If you choose exercise, you will realize there are several events on the journey. It is not enough to do only aerobic exercise—walking, biking, jogging, swimming, dance, etc: Your body needs strength and flexibility as much as it needs endurance. So yoga and weight lifting and tai chi are as important as your walk.

No matter how hard you try, there will always be those unwanted free radicals that will bombard your body and lead to illnesses. Look at Lance Armstrong, the cyclist who won the Tour de France in 1999 and 2000. At the peak of his physical condition, he found he had cancer of the testicles that had spread to his lungs and brain. He certainly had all the physical fitness he needed, but disease occurred anyway. Perhaps all the excess training to be a competitive athlete made him more susceptible to an increase in free radicals and thus disease occurred. It is possible his sense of invincibility led to an imbalance of the mind that suppressed his immune system.

Perhaps even after his victory, Armstrong did not understand how much control he had of his destiny. He wrote a book, *It's Not About the Bike: My Journey Back to Life* (Putnam Publishing, 2000), in which he states, "As I passed into unconsciousness, my doctors controlled my future. For that period of time, they were the ultimate beings. My doctors were my God." His belief that doctors were his god is enough of a mistake to lead to a suppressed immune system. He felt he had no control over his decisions. He felt no control over his health. The statement also implies a poor knowledge of his spiritual self. No human being can ever be your God. It is this lack of spiritual imbalance that can lead to disease.

It is said in the ancient textbooks of India that a mistake of the intellect leads to a change in the vibration of the mind and body. This simple change leads people to forget the perfect health they once had, whereupon disease occurs. Losing harmony with the universe means losing control of health. The vibration of body/mind/soul energy is your tune in nature. You are in balance when all three are in balance. Lance Armstrong had great physical balance, but imbalance of the spirit, and that can lead to illness.

Another aspect of physical balance is to provide the body with antioxidant protection. While it is important that you get plenty of antioxidants from fruits and vegetables, supplements are also necessary. You learned the program on supplements and antioxidants in Chapter 6. Physicians and researchers are realizing that these antioxidants not only prevent but also help to cure certain illnesses. The major sources are vitamins and herbs. So you must add supplements to your program of AGEproofing.

Linus Pauling, Ph.D., studied one of the most important antioxidants, Vitamin C. His research on Vitamin C (Ascorbic Acid) revealed its healing powers in heart disease as well as cancer. Antioxidants are part of your events.

In today's world, the news media have taken stories out of context and confused the public. Don't be swayed by the negative press about antioxidants. Eventually all the thousands of years of practicing natural cures will prevail. Antioxidants are one of the most important steps in AGEproofing.

## The mental realm

The best way to talk about mental attitude is with a story about a patient of mine. The patient, Shirley Snyder, recently shared with me some of the obstacles she has had to deal with in her physical life. She has given me permission to share them with you. Shirley writes in her memoir:

"This is everyday, common sense that can be followed to maintain a healthy immune system, which in turn insures a disease-free body and mind.

"When I was younger, a doctor told me I had asthma. I told him that I did not want asthma and never had another attack. I often wonder what happened to the asthma.

"Over the years I have managed to recover from colon cancer that spread to my liver. I am still alive 12 years later despite the medical profession telling that I had three to six months to live.

"When I was diagnosed with lupus, I made up my mind I was going to put it in remission. I built up my immune system and the symptoms went away. Even though I pretend not to have a hip prosthesis, I am reminded of it when I wear high heels and go to the mall.

"It was easy for me to have a positive attitude about my illnesses, because being an Aries, I always thought that I could do anything, especially when I was challenged. I visualize myself healthy and never doubt it.

"After you get yourself together, do something for someone else. Don't expect anything in return.

"Negative thoughts slowly deteriorate your body and mind. Remember . . . kind words heal; mean words kill."

What you begin to see is that Shirley is on a journey in which her mind affects her body. Negative thoughts are events that can lead to disease, so Shirley eliminates the thought of disease to keep her mind's journey on course.

In her letter to me, she goes on to say much more about her belief system. She believes that attitude, exercise, genetics, alternative medical treatment, environmental safety, and nutrition affect your immune system, and thus your state of good health.

I know there are many books on controlling your mind and thus your health. But when you read about people like Shirley Snyder, you see how knowledge can come directly to an individual. Her story is living proof of a higher power and the healing power of what I call the Apollo Factor.

The mind determines the outcome of so many illnesses. One of the fastest-growing fields of research is psychoneuro-immunology, the study of the effects the mind has on the chemistry of the cells and body. The research clearly points to the fact that your thoughts, your level of stress, and your happiness have everything to do with how you protect yourself from disease.

When an individual comes to my alternative medicine office, the first determination that I make is how they view their disease. How they are dealing with the diagnosis?

Often, even in the face of great adversity, individuals gain insight and strength from their illness. Remember Brad Lundstrom, the young man with the brain tumors who started a support group for people with cancer?

Some of my greatest inspirations have come from individuals who have AIDS. Their spirit often soars. Human beings have a great ability to deal with adversity if they have the right mental outlook. I call this mental outlook their intention. You can see from Shirley Snyder's story that she intends to stay well. The doctor's diagnosis is not going to alter the outcome of her health. She is in charge; her intention directs the outcome.

I find too often that physicians are too negative. One of the differences between alternative physicians and allopathic physicians is their belief system. Alternative physicians believe that all diseases are curable. Allopathic physicians believe that once you make the diagnosis, you look at the statistical probability of improvement. All too often the allopathic system leaves the patient in a state of despair, which in turn has a negative effect on the immune system, and thus adds to the stress of the disease.

The alternative physician's intention to cure all disease is a much better system. It incorporates the healing of the mind, body, and spirit. It brings patients into action and leads them on a different journey. Patients realize that they are in control of their life, not the doctors.

Remember after you read this book that a quiet mind has a direct connection to the true healing of the universe—the quantum healing. Remember that your body is not separate from the universe; it is an extension of the universe. You are a vibration, a wave of energy in a large quantum field. That is why your mind is so important: You can achieve a state of potential healing by changing your cell vibrations. When your cell vibrations are in tune with the universe, spontaneous healing can occur. This is the reason that prayer and meditation have such a profound impact on health. Many mental exercises have an impact on your health. Your intention to get well ranks very high among them.

## The spiritual realm

Beyond the mental however, there is another entire realm of medicine—the spiritual realm. The spirituality of the individual is just beginning to be considered an important aspect of healing and health. It is my prediction that the next great change that will occur in medicine will be for doctors to learn how to become healers, not just practitioners of medicine. In order for this to occur, they will, like all great healers of the past and future, need to understand the importance of the patient's spiritual needs.

I find that the minute I begin to approach the subject of the spirit from a health viewpoint, it makes some people uncomfortable. To be honest, in my thirty years of medicine, I have not always been as open to discussing spirituality with my patients. Now, however, I find it is an essential element in healing. You can work with the body and the mind—that's easy. The conflict comes with the mistaken perceptions that people have about spirit.

Webster defines spirit as the life principle, especially in man. The breath of life. The thinking, motivating, feeling part of man, often as distinguished from the body. The soul. Regarded as separate from matter.

Separate from matter—the breath of life. Imagine your doctor talking to you about your life force. In today's modern approach to health there is no room for the unknown. Doctors are either scientific or they're quacks. The modern approach always dismisses the unknown. Spontaneous healings are errors. Prayer could not possibly work to cure illness. Despite this approach, however, the modern method is a dismal failure. Cancer is on the rise, and AIDS is epidemic. If the medical profession cannot explain disease in a scientific way—chronic fatigue syndrome is an example—then the syndrome just doesn't exist. Try telling this to the thousands and perhaps millions of people who cannot get out of bed and have no explanation for their illness.

The best approach to health is balance. I think it is interesting that most natural forms of healing include some description of a life force. The Chinese call it *chi*, the Japanese call it *Ki*, and the Ayurvedics call it *Prana*, but we in modern western medicine ignore that the life force exists. How arrogant can we be? To ignore the spirituality of healing is to ignore the very essence of man.

The field of quantum physics has verified that the universe contains more space than matter. So too we as humans have more empty space then we do matter. Why concentrate only of the physical side of the healing? There is more going on in the soul of the universe—the unknown space—than we can see. There is more going on in the spirit of man than we can see.

We do not have to think that spirituality requires a certain religious belief. Religion and spirituality can be separate if you choose. My belief in God and creation does not mean that I believe agnostics don't have a spiritual side. We all have a universal consciousness and/or soul awareness. We humans have a spiritual connection. Many of us believe in a higher power and God.

No one has stated it better in my opinion then Deepak Chopra, M.D., in his recent book *How to Know God* (Harmony Books, 2000). Chopra talks about the seven human responses and their identity.

| RESPONSE | IDENTITY IS BASED ON |
| --- | --- |
| Fight-flight | Physical body and environment |
| Reactive | Ego and personality |
| Restful awareness | Silent witness |
| Intuitive | The knower within |
| Creative | Co-creator with God |
| Visionary | Enlightenment |
| Sacred | The source of all |

As you can see, our creative response is a belief in God as creator. The source of all human response is the sacred. Modern medicine is incomplete if it eliminates the source of human responses—the soul.

Dr. Chopra contends that scientific research is incomplete. The brain responds to every phase of spiritual life. I agree with the contention that scientific research is incomplete and that medicine cannot explain spontaneous remissions any more then it can explain where Shirley Snyder's asthma went. It is just not always possible to explain such mysterious remissions at the physical level. They can be explained at a spiritual level—I see such things every day.

Patients have to eventually become more spiritual if their healing is to be complete. It is not enough to be of sound body; you must be of sound mind and sound soul.

There is a song by Clay Walker that says, "Don't let the chain of love end with you." We have to love all other humans and creatures alike if we are going to create a harmonious society. We have to relearn our collective spirituality as humans and tolerate our differences. We have to stop the environmental and the social disasters from occurring by raising our consciousness to bring about the perfect health of mind and body and soul.

I have made many transitions in my career. But if you were to ask me, "What is the greatest lesson you have learned?" my answer would be, "The quest for the spiritual, my belief that the spiritual transcends the physical body." To become a healer, the physician must have a quiet mind. It is in silence that the knowledge to become a healer is found. All healing comes from a higher power, and the physician is simply the tool to healing!

I started my life as a little boy on the streets of Newark, New Jersey. You have to believe that anything is possible when you look at how I started and the the career that I have had. I started by having parents who taught me the value of family, hard work, and a belief in God. From my early beginnings it was evident that being of sound physical body took hard work. The world of athletics taught me how to live with disappointment and bounce back, how a physically sound body can improve the function of the mind.

But it was the mind that directed the outcome of the

body. The technique of meditation has been the most helpful learning tool that I could have ever imagined. Why? Because it has put me in touch with the universal knowledge and has made me aware that I am an extension of a higher power. I am not the healer. I am the person selected to teach others how to heal.

It is said in Ayurvedic medicine, "If you want to know the state of the mind yesterday, look at the body today." The most scientific approaches to health are not always the best. We as humans are not scientific experiments! We are the creation of a higher power. It is our spiritual nature and soul awareness that makes us unique.

We have similar bodies to others. We have similar minds to others. But we have uniqueness of spirit. We have different vibrations that keep the universe in balance. This balance obviously cannot be the work of our bodies or minds, so it must be our souls, our spirits, that are unique. It is that uniqueness that will eventually lead to better health and longevity.

So while I hope you will begin your journey with AGE-proofing as your guide to the steps to health and longevity, remember that the next great advance in health will come from the effect of human spirit, and that will be the next lesson I will teach you.

Keep me in your prayers, and I will keep you in mine. Thank you for sharing *AGEproofing* with me.

Robert D. Willix Jr., M.D., F.A.C.S.M.

# Bibliography

Ames, B.N., "DNA damage by endogenous oxidants in mitogenesis as causes of aging in cancer," *Molecular Biology of Free Radical Scavenging Systems,* Cold Spring Harbor Laboratory Press, Planeview, 1992, 1-21.

"The Biology and Physiology of Aging," *The Western Journal of Medicine,* December 1990.

Calaprice, Alice, ed. *The Quotable Einstein,* Princeton University Press, 1996.

Cameron, E, M.D., et al, "Innovations vs. quality control, an unpublishable clinical trial of supplemental ascorbate in incurable cancer," *Medical Hypothesis,* v. 36, 1991, 185-189.

"Can Vitamins Help?" *Consumer Reports,* January 1992.

Chopra, Deepak. *Ageless Body, Timeless Mind,* Crown Publishers, Harmony Books, 1993.

—. *Creating Health,* Hougton, Mifflin, 1991.

—. *Quantum Healing,* Bantam New Age, 1989.
"Complementary Self-Care Strategies for Healthy Aging," *Generations,* Fall 1993.

Chowka, Peter Barry. "Interview with Dr. Linus Pauling," Nutrition Science News, April 1996.

Cooper, Kenneth. *The Aerobics Way,* Harmony Books, 1994.

Cooper, Kenneth H., M.D., M.P.H., *Advanced Nutritional Therapies,* Thomas Nelson Publisher, 1996.

Digiesi, V., et al, "Coenzyme Q10 in essential hypertension," *Molecular Aspects Medicine Supplement 253 to 257,* 1994.

Eliot, Robert. *A Change of heart: Converting Your Stresses to Strengths,* Bantam Books, 1993.

Eliot, Robert, and Dennis Breo. *Is it Worth Dying For? A Self-Assessment Program to Make Stress Work for You, Not Against You,* Bantam Books, 1989.

"Explaining Fruit Fly Longevity," *Science,* June 11, 1993.

"Good Sense, Good Health," *Sports Illustrated*, November 13, 1989.

Hewitt, James. *Teach Yourself Yoga*, NTC Publishing Group, 1993.

Hittleman, Richard. *Yoga for Health*, Ballantine Books, 1985.

"How Long Is the Human Life-Span?" *Science*, November 15, 1991.

"In Search of Methuselah: Estimating the Upper Limits to Human Longevity," *Science*, November 2, 1990.

*Journal of Advancement in Medicine*, Winter 1993.

Kagan, V.E., et al, "The universal antioxidant in the membrane in the aqueous phase," *Biochemical Pharmacologie*, v. 44, 1992, 1637-1649.

Kasch, Fred W. *Adult Fitness, Principles & Practice*, Mayfield Publishers, 1968.

Kriegel, Robert, and Marilyn Kriegel. *The C-Zone*, Fawcett, 1985.

Kronhausen, E., et al, Formula for Life, William Morrow and Co., New York, 1989, p. 77.

Leske, M.C., et al. "Antioxidant vitamins and nuclear opacities: the longitudinal study of cataract," *Ophthalmology*, May 1998, v. 105, 831-6.

"Living Longer," *Men's Health*, Spring 1989.

Maharishi Maheesh Yogi. *Transcendental Meditation: Science of Being and Art of Living*, NAL–Dutton, 1988.

"Mighty Vitamins," *Medical World News*, January 1993.

"Mighty Vitamins," *Medical World News*, January 1993.

"Mind-Survival Link Emerges From Death Data," *Science News*, November 6, 1993.

Murray, Michael T., N.D. *The Encyclopedia of Nutritional Supplements*, Prima Publishing, 1996.

Nader, Tony, M.D., Ph.D., *Human Physiology, Expression of Veda and the Vedic Literature*, Maharishi Vedic University, Vlodrop, The Netherlands,1995.

Niwa, Y., et al. *Saishinigaku,* Japan, 38, 1983, 1450-1458.

Passwater, Richard A., Ph.D. "Interview with Dr Denhem Harman," *Whole Foods* magazine (WFC Inc.).

Perls, Thomas, M.D., M.P.H., F.A.C.P. Harvard Division on Aging, Beth Israel Deaconess Medical Center, Cambridge, MA,. Interview published in *Reuters Press Report,* March 15, 1998.

"Phenomena, Comment and Notes," *Smithsonian,* May 1990.

Portugues, Gladys, and Joyce Vedral. *Hard Bodies,* Dell Publishing, 1986.

Prassad, K.N., et al. "High doses of multiple antioxidant vitamins essential ingredients in improving the efficacy of standard cancer therapy," *Journal of the American College of Nutrition,* February 1999, 18:1, 13-25.

"Protein Oxidation and Aging," *Science,* August 28, 1992.

Purdy, Judy, "Hale and hearty at 100," Research report from the Office of the Vice-President for Research at the University of Georgia, Summer 1995.

Quillon, P., and R. M. Williams, eds. *Adjuvant Nutrition in Cancer Treatment,* Cancer Treatment Research Foundation, 1993.

Russell, Peter. *The TM Technique: An Introduction to Transcendental Meditation and the Teachings of Maharishi Maheesh Yogi,* Viking-Penguin, 1989.

Sears, Barry. "Essential Fatty Acids and Dietary Endocrinology: A Hypothesis for Cardiovascular Treatment," *The Journal of Advancement in Medicine,* Vol. 6, No. 4, Human Sciences Press Inc., 1993.

Seyle, Hans. *Stress Without Distress,* NAL–Dutton, 1975.

Shamberger, R.J., et al. *Archives of Environmental Health,*Vol. 31, 1976, 231-35.

Sharma, Hari. *Freedom From Disease,* Atrium Books, 1992.

Sharma, Hari, M.D. *Freedom From Disease,* Veda Publishing, 1993.

Sinatra, Stephen T., M.D. *Heartbreak: A Mind-Body Prescription for Healing the Heart,* Keats Publishing, 1996.

Sivananda Yoga Center. *Sivananda Companion to Yoga*, New York: Simon and Schuster, 1983.

"Slow Forward," *American Health: Fitness of Body and Mind*, July-August 1989.

Sprague, Ken. *The Gold's Gym Book of Weight Training*, Perigee Books, 1993.

"Survival of the Fittest," *Health*, May-June 1993.

"The Three Secrets of Shangri-la," *In Health*, July-August 1990.

"Toward a New Image of Aging," *Prevention Magazine*, June 1990.

"Unfit Survivors: Exercise as a Resource for Aging Women," *The Gerontologist*, June 1991.

*Vecchia, C., et al. "Tea consumption in cancer risk,"* Nutritional Cancer, v. 17, 1992, 27-31.

"Vitamin C Intake and Longer Life," *The Washington Post*, May 11, 1992, A2.

Yu, S.Y., et al. *Biologic Trace Element Research*, January 1997, v. 56:1, 117-124.

"The War on Aging," *Life*, October 1992.

"Why Do We Age?" *Scientific American*, December 1992.

Willix, Robert. *Stress Management for the Business Executive* (privately published paper), 1992.

"Working Out Shapes Up to a Longer Life," *USA Today*, February 25, 1993, A2.

Zebroff, Kareen. *Back Fitness the Yoga Way*, Gordon Boules Books, 1989.